BEOWULF

BEOWULF

TRANSLATED BY
KEVIN CROSSLEY-HOLLAND

AND INTRODUCED BY
BRUCE MITCHELL

FARRAR, STRAUS & GIROUX

New York

CONTENTS

TRANSLATOR'S NOTE

In my first week at Oxford I came across the rather beautiful Old English riddle about a swan. I remember that I tried to translate it, and failed. I failed my Old English exams too, at the end of my second term. That meant some hours of the summer term should be given over to work; and in a way they were, though I felt already the force of the *Beowulf* poet's philosophy: *Gæð a wyrd swa hio scel*, or, roughly, whatever will be will be.

On a soft evening shortly before resitting that vital exam I was in a moored punt with a friend, a pork pie, and my grammar when a swan attacked me. It was hardly a matter of 'a sudden blow' or of 'great wings beating', but sufficient none the less to inspire terror. I leaped for the bank and landed in hospital with a torn cartilage. To that swan, I am quite sure, which offered me ten hygienic days with so little to distract, I owed my continuing presence in the University.

In my last term I came across that riddle again, and again tried to translate it. This time there was something to show for it:

> Silent is my dress when I step across the earth,
> Reside in my house, or ruffle the waters.
> Sometimes my adornments and this high windy air
> Lift me over the livings of men,
> The power of the clouds carries me far
> Over all people. My white pinions
> Resound very loudly, ring with a melody,
> Sing out clearly, when I sleep not on
> The soil or settle on grey waters . . . a travelling spirit.

These lines, the first I had translated from Old English, add up in the original to an elegant, highly-wrought little diversion (though not to much of a riddle); they curiously foreshadow,

as Edward Lucie-Smith has pointed out, a famous poem by
Yeats — not, of course, the poem about Leda's rapacious swan,
brother to those that float on the Cherwell, but 'The Wild
Swans at Coole'.

Although I had no taste for learning the mechanics of the
language, the mood of much Old English poetry had attracted
me immediately; and my sympathy with it has seemed to grow
from day to day. Sometimes passionate, often sorrowful,
occasionally wry, but always stoic, formal, and highly sophisticated, the voice of the Old English poets is absolutely distinc-
tive. Theirs was a poetry born of a chill, unfriendly world
peopled by warrior bands, where loyalty was the greatest virtue
and life an endless struggle against meaningless fate. The Saxon
warrior's attitude to life is nicely summed up in the Norse
proverb, 'One thing I know never dies nor changes, the reputation of a dead man', and it is pertinent that the last word of
Beowulf describes that hero as *lofgeornost*, 'most eager for fame'.
The Germanic code is, of course, fundamental to Old English
poetry, but in time the traditional and pagan themes came to
be balanced by the new, hopeful, and Christian. It was not
always a matter of old *or* new. The two were sometimes strik-
ingly fused within a single poem, just as the helmet found at
Benty Grange bears both the pagan boar and the Christian
cross. The best of the Old English poets responded powerfully
to this changing world and should arouse a powerful response
in us.

They have not really done so; and it is not difficult to see
why Old English poetry is so little known, so often underrated.
First, Old English has to be learnt; most of us, with no time
for this, must have recourse to translation; and what translations we have, with a few exceptions, are rather inadequate.
Secondly, although every inch of Old English poetry has been
subjected to close textual examination, it has not received its
due share of sensible critical evaluation. Thirdly, its inclusion
in university English syllabuses is often questioned, sometimes
openly condemned. But that does not mean that some Old
English poems are not great and imaginative works of art.

The act of translating *Beowulf* calls for no apologia. It is by
far the finest poem in the relatively small canon — about
30,000 lines — of Old English poetry. More important, it is a
poem of tremendous power and range, the work of a man
(most probably a Christian) fully able to carry out what I take
to be his purpose: the depiction of an ideal Germanic hero
within the framework of a gripping, human story. Those who
come to *Beowulf* for the first time, perhaps expecting it to be
remote, may be surprised by the essentially English character
of the poem. For if the society reflected in it now seems alien,
many of its moods are wholly familiar: an out-and-out heroism,
a dogged refusal to surrender, a love of the sea, an enjoyment
of melancholy, nostalgia. *Beowulf* has the power to stir us to
the roots of our being; through it, we can come to understand
more about our origins, and thus achieve a deeper sense of
perspective. It will not be enough to 'taste' a page here and a
page there; much of the poem's strength lies in accumulative
impact.

I should perhaps note here the principles I have followed in
attempting this translation. My staple diet has been a non-
syllabic four-stress line, controlled by light alliteration. There
are plenty of cases, though, where I have not conformed to
this pattern; my concern has been to echo rather than slavishly
to imitate the original. My diction inclines towards the formal,
though it is certainly less formal than that of the *Beowulf* poet;
it seemed to me important at this time to achieve a truly acces-
sible version of the poem, that eschewed the use of archaisms,
inverted word orders, and all 'poetic' language. I have not
gone out of my way to avoid words that spring from Latin
roots, but the emphasis has fallen naturally on words derived
from Old English. This translation is, we believe, by and large
faithful to the letter of the original, but it is the mood that I
have been after. And if I have not caught anything of it, then
I have not succeeded in my purpose. I have worked from C. L.
Wrenn's edition of the poem. The same scholar's revision of
John R. Clark Hall's prose translation was my undergraduate
stand-by and now and then, sometimes consciously, some-

times unconsciously, I have used a phrase of his which could not be bettered. Finally, I must add that I believe this translation should be read out loud — an epic in the oral tradition is never going to sit very easily on the printed page.

I have many to thank. First, I sincerely thank my wife, who has made many valuable comments; she has weathered the word-storm with patience and understanding. I thank, too, Professor Burton Raffel, translator of *Beowulf,* and Professor Joseph Clancy, for their friendly encouragement from across the Atlantic; George MacBeth for his private and public support; Helen May for her enthusiasm and assistance; Jill Paton Walsh for textual assistance; Brigitte Hanf for her very fine drawings. Then I thank my father for his extensive and always helpful comments, and Mario Rinvolucri for his quite remarkable generosity in devoting an entire week to a rigorous reading of what I thought was my finished typescript. Above all, I thank Bruce Mitchell, who has given me so much scholarly advice both textual and critical during the past four years. This is the second book we have done together, and we are able to countenance the thought of a third!

KEVIN CROSSLEY-HOLLAND

Finsbury
April 1968

INTRODUCER'S NOTE

I **WANT** first to express my thanks to the many scholars and pupils from whose writings or conversation about *Beowulf* I have (or should have) profited. The Rev. H. E. J. Cowdrey and Mr. Edward Wilson, both of St. Edmund Hall, deserve special mention here.

Acknowledgements are due, and are gratefully made, to the authors, editors, and publishers, of those books and journals from which I have quoted. I thank particularly Macmillan and Co. Ltd. and St. Martin's Press Inc. for permission to reprint *The Finnesburh Fragment* (Appendix I) and several passages of comment from *The Battle of Maldon and Other Old English Poems*; the Editorial Board of *Neophilologus* for permission to use or reprint portions of my article ' "Until the Dragon Comes . . . ": Some Thoughts on *Beowulf*', which appeared in *Neophilologus* 47 (1963), 126–138; and Professor J. R. R. Tolkien for permission to quote from a cherished private letter.

I am conscious of deep obligations to Professor Keith Macartney of Melbourne, who introduced me to *Beowulf*, and to Professors J. R. R. Tolkien, C. L. Wrenn, and A. Campbell, for the lectures I have heard them deliver and the stimulus I have derived from them.

Thanks are also due to the translator (we have spent many happy hours working together) and his wife, to Mrs. E. M. Crampton of Oxford, and to my wife, for valuable assistance while this work was in progress. My debt to my mother is acknowledged with gratitude in the dedication.

BRUCE MITCHELL

Oxford
December 1967

The map is based on that in Klaeber's edition of *Beowulf* by kind permission of George G. Harrap and Company. The names of the less important tribes are given in upper and lower case.

The village of Lejre (south-west of Roskilde on the island of Zealand) is often identified with the seat of the Scylding Kings. It has been marked as the site of Heorot.

INTRODUCTION

1. *Attitudes to* Beowulf

Beowulf is a poem. One of the most pleasing trends in recent Old English studies has been an increasing awareness of the truth and importance of this simple observation. But it is one which has often been overlooked by scholars and critics, some of whom have preferred to regard *Beowulf* as a museum for the antiquarian, a sourcebook for the historian, a treatise for the student of Christian thought, or a gymnasium for the philologist. Those who have treated it as one of these things have helped the Grendel of criticism to devour the poem in the presence of generations of students. Other teachers and writers, in a laudable but excessive reaction, have swung too far the other way and have made somewhat extravagant claims about the place of *Beowulf* in English literature.

In his brilliant British Academy Lecture of 1936, J. R. R. Tolkien gave an amusing and cogent summary of the bewildering variety of theories about the *Beowulf* poet's ideas and aims. He said:

. . . we must pass in rapid flight over the heads of many decades of critics. As we do so a conflicting babel mounts up to us, which I can report as something after this fashion. 'Beowulf is a half-baked native epic the development of which was killed by Latin learning; it was inspired by emulation of Virgil, and is a product of the education that came in with Christianity; it is feeble and incompetent as a narrative; the rules of narrative are cleverly observed in the manner of the learned epic; it is the confused product of a committee of muddle-headed and probably beer-bemused Anglo-Saxons (this is a Gallic voice); it is a string of pagan lays edited by monks; it is the work of a learned but inaccurate Christian antiquarian; it is a work of genius, rare and surprising in the period, though the genius seems to have been shown principally in doing something much better left undone (this is a very recent voice); it is a wild folk-tale (general chorus); it is a poem of an aristocratic and courtly tradition (same voices); it is a hotch-potch; it is a sociological, anthropological, archaeological document; it is a mythical allegory (very old voices these and generally shouted down, but not so far out as some of the newer cries); it is rude and rough; it is a masterpiece of metrical art; it has no shape at all; it is singularly weak in construction; it is a clever allegory of contemporary politics (old John Earle with some slight support from Mr. Girvan, only they look to different periods); its architecture is solid; it is thin and cheap (a solemn voice); it is undeniably weighty (the same voice); it is a national epic; it is a translation from the Danish; it was imported by Frisian traders; it is a burden to English syllabuses; and (final universal chorus of all voices) it is worth studying.'

A subsequent generation of scholars has increased the confusion by giving new twists to old theories and by producing new ones. Thus we learn from one writer that *Beowulf* was composed for a 'fit audience . . ., though few' by an ivory-towered poet of the eighth century and from another that it is a soldering-together of three orally-composed lays which were originally independent. One sees in it a Christian allegory of Salvation,* while others seem to have found something very akin to the modern cult of the anti-hero and argue that the poem contains criticism or even condemnation of Beowulf's actions while he was king.

Clearly there is something peculiar about a poem which produces such a wild variety of reactions. It is at least in part a failure of communication. This is not the poet's fault but the result of our ignorance of the conventions within which Anglo-Saxon poems were written. We do not know who wrote *Beowulf*, or by whom, when, and where, it was first heard. What the author took for granted in his audience we can never determine with any accuracy. Let us reverse the roles. Imagine

* These writers are respectively P. F. Baum, F. P. Magoun, Jr., and M. B. McNamee.

King Alfred suddenly transported to the cinema or the Vener-
able Bede placed in front of a television set to look at a series
of Perry Mason stories. We can suppose that Bede might be
convinced by the ritualistic nature of the offerings that he was
watching a religious rite designed to placate some twentieth-
century god. He might even detect in them allegories of the
struggle between right and wrong. We can recognize our
dilemma in his.

Some modern critics fail to do this. Consciously or unconsciously they take for granted fundamental assumptions which
cannot be proven and erect on these elaborate theories which
cannot be tested. Not all admit that their foundations are
assumptions. Some seem self-hypnotized and unaware of the
dangers of what has been condemned as 'a tendency to
speculate on the things that are not expressed in *Beowulf*'.
Others demonstrate what might be called a tendency to identify
themselves with the *Beowulf* poet and to assume that their
speculations have at last revealed what the poet had in mind.
A little more humility in the face of our basic ignorance
would do some of us no harm.

2. *Summary of the Poem* ★

LINES 1–2199. YOUNG BEOWULF IN DENMARK

1. *The fight with Grendel*

Lines 1–188. The story of Scyld, the founder of the Scylding
(Danish) dynasty. The building of Heorot by the Danish king
Hrothgar. The attacks of Grendel.

Lines 189–661. Beowulf's voyage to Denmark, his reception,
and the feast in the hall.

Lines 662–836. Beowulf's watch for Grendel. Grendel's approach. The fight and Beowulf's victory.

★ I am indebted to Fr. Klaeber's edition of *Beowulf* for the basic arrange-
ment of this summary. A sequential retelling of the fight between Beowulf
and the dragon will be found in 'Beowulf's Fight with the Dragon' by
Kenneth Sisam in *Review of English Studies* 9 (1958), 129–140. For details of
the episodes and digressions, see Appendix V.

Lines 2711–2820. Beowulf's death.

Lines 2821–3030. The announcement of Beowulf's death.

Lines 3030–3136. The recovery of the treasure and the preparations for the funeral.

Lines 3137–3182. Beowulf's funeral and the dirge.

3. *Manuscript and Date and Place of Composition*

Beowulf survives only in the British Museum Cotton Vitellius A.xv, a manuscript which was damaged, but fortunately not destroyed, by the fire which in 1731 swept through the Cottonian collection of manuscripts. A few words were lost from many pages and some damage was done by crumbling of the burnt edges before the folios were remounted and rebound, perhaps some time in the 1860s. The most badly damaged parts of the manuscript were those containing *Beowulf*. Again fortunately, we have the two Thorkelin transcripts of *Beowulf* made in 1786–1787, one by an unknown copyist, the other by the Icelander Thorkelin, the first editor of the poem. The manuscript also contains a 350-line fragment of the poem *Judith* (a Jewish 'saints' life' based on the Vulgate story) and some prose texts which (like *Beowulf*) deal with monsters and marvels.

No exact date can be given for the composition of the poem. The manuscript itself was probably written about 1000. The mention of the death of Hygelac — the historical Chlochilaichus of the *Historia Francorum* of Gregory of Tours — who was killed in a raid on the Frisian territory of the Franks *c.* 521, gives us an earlier limit. But other historical evidence suggests that the earliest date is after *c.* 680, when Germanic alliterative verse began to be used for Christian purposes. Some have argued that, since the poem glorifies the Danes, it is unlikely to have been written after *c.* 835, when the Danish raids on Anglo-Saxon England began in grim earnest. Others, for various reasons, plead for a date later in the ninth century or even at the end of it. Examination of the language can do little more than confirm the possibility that the poem was composed between *c.* 680 and 800 (or perhaps later).

We do not know where or for whom the poem was composed. If we opt for Northumbria in the time of Bede, we shall assign its composition to the period *c.* 680–730. If we take it to be a product of the Mercian court during the time of Mercia's supremacy, we shall plump for a date later in the eighth century — Offa ruled from 757 to 796. The possibility that the poem was composed in East Anglia was not, I think, seriously entertained until the discovery of the Sutton Hoo Ship Burial in 1939 revealed the existence of an East Anglian civilization which knew the armour, weapons, and jewels, so lovingly described in *Beowulf*. Now a number of scholars are inclined to think that the poem may have been composed in the court of an East Anglian king in the late seventh or early eighth century.

Unless some startling discovery is made, the date and the place of *Beowulf*'s composition are unlikely to be more accurately determined.

4. *The Authorship of* Beowulf

Is *Beowulf* as we have it the work of one poet only? The proper answer to this question (which was disregarded in the discussion about when and where the poem was composed) is 'We don't know.' But since our critical attitude to *Beowulf* may to some extent depend on whether we reply 'Yes' or 'No', a brief examination of the possible answers seems justified.

According to Fr. Klaeber, 'the poem of *Beowulf* consists of two distinct parts joined in a very loose manner and held together only by the person of the hero. The first of these does not in the least require or presuppose a continuation. Nor is the second dependent for its interpretation on the events of the first plot. . . .' This is so obviously true — on the surface at any rate — that many early views of the poem took for granted its composite nature. Thus Benjamin Thorpe in 1855 wrote: 'I do not hesitate to regard it as a Christian paraphrase of a heathen Saga, and those [Christian] allusions as interpolations of the paraphrast, whom I conceive to have been a native of England of Scandinavian parentage.' Since then, the view that *Beowulf* is a Christian reworking of a pagan poem has found powerful advocates. Thus H. M. Chadwick, writing in 1912, claimed that 'the great bulk of the poem must have been in existence — not merely as a collection of lays or stories, but in full epic form — an appreciable time before the middle of the seventh century'. This epic was adapted for a Christian audience. The adapting poet was not deeply versed in Christianity; hence the Christian references are elementary.

Others have gone further in dissecting the poem. Karl Müllenhoff in 1869 separated it into six parts, each by a different man — he identified two original poets, a continuator, an introducer, and two interpolators. More recently, F. P. Magoun, Jr., was led by his (in my opinion unjustified) belief that the poem must have been orally composed to divide it into three originally separate lays — the first fights, the recapitulation at Hygelac's court, and the dragon fight.

The view perhaps most current today is that *Beowulf* was composed in its present form by one poet who may or may not have inherited the plot ready-made. But there is nothing which compels us to accept this assumption, and, even if we do, we are by no means out of the wood; there are still many ways of interpreting the poem. The question posed at the beginning of this section is insoluble, but if we follow Kenneth Sisam's example we shall not be unduly embarrassed by this: 'I deal with the structure of the poem as it stands in MS. Vitellius A.xv, copied round about the year 1000, assuming that its text represents approximately the form given to the story by one man — original poet, or poet-editor, or accomplished reciter able to adapt and vary existing stories in verse.' From now on, we shall call this 'one man' the '*Beowulf* poet'.

5. The Aims of the Beowulf Poet

The only evidence we have for these is the poem, a poem which is unique in the sense that no other Old English poem like it has survived. It seems reasonable to believe that one of the aims of the author was to entertain — we have sea-

monsters, man-eating giants, and a fire-spouting dragon, alongside human kings and warriors; we have fighting and treasure,
blood and jewels. Many modern critics agree that the poem
was intended for oral recitation in a secular hall, though they
disagree about how Christian the audience was. Some, however, claim that the poem was meant to be recited or read to a
monastic audience, while others think that it was written for a
lone reader in cell or bower. Few, however, would deny that
the poet had some idea of somehow entertaining somebody.

Whether or not he also intended to teach, it is clear that no
Germanic warrior could have come to any harm from hearing
the poem. We have in it a portrayal of the heroic way of living
and thinking from which we can understand the responsi-
bilities, privileges, and ideals, of warriors and leaders from
youth to old age.

In common with many other Old English poems, *Beowulf*
is much concerned with this transient life, with 'grief after
joy' (line 1775). J. R. R. Tolkien has said: 'It is an heroic-
elegiac poem; and in a sense all its first 3,136 lines are the pre-
lude to a dirge.'

However, the didactic and elegiac strands may be merely
incidental. As Kenneth Sisam writes: 'If the poem is considered
as entertainment for a hall-company, diversity of mood is one
of its great merits; and in this quality no other Anglo-Saxon
poem that has come down to us is comparable.' The same
writer forces us to ask ourselves the fundamental question: are
we dealing with a poet concerned primarily with story-telling
and entertainment or with a highly conscious artist who has
written a complex and carefully-constructed poem full of
subtle links, cross-references, and allusions?

We do not know the answer to this and probably never shall.
So each reader will have to find his own answer. Since it is
clear from the account of Beowulf's fight with Grendel that
the poet could tell a straightforward story well, some think
it reasonable to infer from a comparison of his handling
of the fight at Finnesburh (lines 1068–1159) with the way the
same subject is treated in the *Fragment* (see Appendices I and

Ve) that story-telling was not his primary purpose. If it was, the so-called 'digressions' — the mention of Sigemund and Heremod, the Finn Episode, the Heathobard–Danish conflict, the Swedish–Danish wars — are there merely to add interest and variety to the entertainment and we shall agree with Kenneth Sisam that 'this kind of poetry depended on expression, not on silence, dark hints or subtle irony'.

In that case, the point of the Sigemund reference is to compliment Beowulf by comparing him to the greatest of Germanic heroes. That is all. No hint is intended by the poet that the Beowulf now standing in triumph after his defeat of Grendel must, like Sigemund (or perhaps his son), meet his dragon — a dragon which, in Beowulf's case, will be the direct cause of his death. If, on the other hand, we accept the highly sophisticated poet, there is no limit to the ingenuity critics credit him with. While I agree with Kenneth Sisam that some go too far, I think he erred when he wrote: 'That dramatic irony was used in Anglo-Saxon heroic poetry is an assumption. Where it has been detected, the Ango-Saxon audience is supposed to have known something conjectured by a modern critic.' Two examples in *Beowulf* come to mind. In lines 81–85, with the newly-built Heorot towering in all its pride and magnificence, the poet remarks that

> fierce tongues of hateful fire
> had not yet attacked it,

thereby informing (or reminding) his audience that the hall was to be destroyed by fire. He tells them this; there is no need for conjecture by a modern critic. Similarly, after describing the beautiful necklace which is given to Beowulf, the poet tells his audience that Hygelac wore it when he fell in battle (lines 1195 ff.).

We are thus, I think, at liberty to believe in a somewhat more sophisticated poet than the mere teller of tales. But we must beware of making extravagant claims on his behalf and we cannot insist that others believe in him. If we accept him, what aim has he other than mere entertainment? Does he intend to give us a view of man, of his life, and of his place in the universe? If so, what view? There is a bewildering variety of answers to these questions; the Preacher's observation that 'there is no new thing under the sun' does not seem to apply here. Which particular answer we choose to adopt will depend (among other things) on our attitude to two other problems — 'the nature of the monsters' and 'How Christian a poem is *Beowulf*?'

6. *The Nature of the Monsters*

Are Grendel, his mother, and the dragon, anything more than 'commonplaces', 'old wives' tales', the proper matter of 'easy-going romances of chivalry, and of fairy tales'? (These are all phrases used by W. P. Ker, whose main complaint about *Beowulf* was that it put these irrelevancies at the centre and neglected the tragic situations which are the real stuff of poetry.) Many writers have claimed that they are more. The most usual view is that they are Foes of God — a view not hard to defend for Grendel and his mother, since the poet tells us that they are descendants of Cain, whom God drove far away from men for his sin in slaying his brother Abel, and since he actually calls Grendel 'God's adversary'. Kenneth Sisam has issued a caveat: 'The monsters Beowulf kills are inevitably evil and hostile because a reputation for heroism is not made by killing creatures that are believed to be harmless or beneficent — sheep for instance. So the fact that the monsters are evil does not require or favour the explanation that, in the poet's design, they are symbols of evil.' However, the poet has made Grendel and his mother something more than 'ordinary' monsters by choosing to make them foes of God as well as of man.

But what of the dragon? If he is of the same kind as Grendel, why was Beowulf unable to defeat him too? To this question the usual answer is that Beowulf has lost the favour of God. Attempts to explain why have given rise to theories that Beowulf was being criticized by the poet. To some, however, the dragon is a foe of a different kind. Can he, they ask, be death, the foe no man can overcome until death is swallowed up in victory? He need not be an allegorical figure. He is the instrument of Beowulf's death and, as J. R. R. Tolkien has it, 'the placing of the dragon is inevitable: a man can but die upon his death-day'.

If this view is accepted, the problem of why Beowulf had forfeited God's favour disappears. Beowulf in his youth overcomes his foes with God's help. But even with God at his side (lines 2794–2798 and 2874–2876), Beowulf, like all men, must die. Whether this leaves us with a feeling of hope or despair depends in part on our answer to the question 'How Christian a poem is *Beowulf*?'

7. *Christianity in* Beowulf

How Christian is *Beowulf*? Is its Christianity unlearned or learned, very new or well-established, cold, lukewarm, or fervent? Indeed, what is Christian about it?

That the Church was prepared to baptize what it could not suppress is clear from Pope Gregory's letter to Mellitus, quoted by Bede (i. 30), where Mellitus is urged to sanctify the pagan shrines after destroying the idols and is advised to hold solemn feasts of a Christian sort using the oxen which in the past would have been sacrificed to idols. Similarly, we find pagan concepts Christianized. *Lof* — fame on the lips of mortal men which warriors won by brave deeds against temporal foes — becomes fame among the angels and happiness in heaven which is won by good deeds and by bravery against the Devil. *Wyrd* 'what happens' (presumably once a pagan concept of blind fate, though it occurs only in post-Christian texts where it throws no real light on Anglo-Saxon pagan beliefs) also seems to have undergone conversion of a sort; the Old English version of *The Consolations of Boethius* says: '*Wyrd* therefore allots to all things their forms, places, seasons, and proportions; but *Wyrd* comes from the mind and forethought of Almighty God.'

The effect of the Christian message must have varied then, as it does today, from individual to individual. To some, conversion must have been a deep and lasting experience. To others, such as the followers of Peada, son of Penda (Bede iii. 21), or the Danes conquered by Alfred (Anglo-Saxon Chronicle 878), it seems to have been an easy shift for reasons of convenience from a not very vital paganism to what was perhaps a tenuously-held belief in a formal Christianity which made little real impact on the heroic outlook. To some, earthly warfare became irreconcilable with the new faith. Bede (iii. 18) tells of King Sigbert of East Anglia, who entrusted his kingdom to a kinsman and, entering a monastery, devoted his energies to winning an everlasting kingdom. When forced out of the monastery into battle in 635, he perished rather than fight. Ælfric has a similar story about a later king of East Anglia, Edmund, who in 869 threw away his weapons when confronted by his Danish foes because he wished to imitate Christ. Even if we think these stories later sophistications and believe that these kings actually died sword in hand, we can see that for some churchmen at any rate there was a stark contrast between the Christian warfare of the monastery — the life of the soldier of Christ — and earthly battle against temporal foes. But this did not hold for all. King Oswald of Northumbria, 'a devout king' of 'ardent faith', fought to save his country (Bede iii. 2). So too did King Alfred and some of his churchmen; the Anglo-Saxon Chronicle for 871 records the death in battle of Bishop Heahmund. And what of the ordinary warrior? To what extent was the heroic code he held influenced by Christian ideas? The *comitatus* duty of loyalty to one's lord survived the coming of Christianity. Miss Dorothy Whitelock has pointed out that the *Penitential of Archbishop Theodore* (died 690) put homicide at a lord's command on a level with killing in battle as an act which demanded only a slight penance and has shown that some churchmen accepted killing for the sake of vengeance until the middle of the eleventh century. As J. R. R. Tolkien wrote to me in a private letter, 'I think we fail to grasp imaginatively the pagan "heroic" temper, the almost animal pride and ferocity of "nobles" and champions on the one hand; or on the other the immense relief and hope of Christian ethical teaching amidst a world with savage values.'

All this suggests that we must be prepared to meet at times a mixture of pagan and Christian concepts and attitudes, a mixture which often we shall not be able to disentangle. There is evidence of relapses to paganism. Bede tells us (iii. 30) how the East Saxons were visited by the plague in 665 and began to renew the heathen shrines which stood desolate, and to worship idols, as if these would protect them from death. The ease of their reconversion by Bishop Jarman suggests that neither faith was very vitally held. Egbert, Archbishop of York 732–766, provided penances for those who made offerings to demons and barred from the priesthood those who worshipped idols. So when we read in lines 175–188 of *Beowulf* that, as Grendel began his ravages, the Danes in Heorot turned from the *scop*'s song of Creation to the worship of idols, we can accept this as portraying an incident possible in England in the poet's time. We shall be troubled only if we believe with A. G. Brodeur that *Beowulf* was composed in an effectively converted England. Has there ever been such a place?

In considering what is Christian about *Beowulf*, we also need to remember that there was a less critical attitude to marvels and wonders. There might be a dragon round the corner; according to the Anglo-Saxon Chronicle, some flew over Northumbria in 793 — portents of the Danish invasions when seen with hindsight. The stories of miracles told in the Lives of Saints also emphasize the gulf between Christians of Anglo-Saxon England and those of today in this respect.

Moreover, there seem to have been different attitudes to pagan literature. In 796 Alcuin wrote his well-known letter to the Bishop of Lindisfarne: 'When priests dine together, let the words of God be read. It is fitting on such occasions to listen to a reader, not to a harpist, to the discourses of the fathers, not to the poems of the heathen. What has Ingeld to do with Christ? The house is narrow; there is no room for both.' Here Alcuin seems to be suggesting that no reconciliation was possible between pagan and Christian poetry. Elsewhere, however, we find him taking a different line. More than once, he uses the proverbial 'gold from dung' image, citing St. Jerome and the Apostle Paul as authorities for the view that gold found in the dung-heap of pagan poetry should be incorporated into the treasure of the Lord and transformed into the riches of ecclesiastical wisdom. We are therefore bound to concede the possibility that a Christian poet might use pagan material.

We can now return to our question 'What is Christian in *Beowulf*?' If we mean obviously and unambiguously Christian, the answer is 'Nothing.' Suppose the only evidence from any source about the religion of Anglo-Saxon England was *Beowulf*, suppose that we had no evidence from history, archaeology, our vocabulary, or anywhere else, that Christian missionaries came to England before 1066, would we be able to prove beyond doubt that the Anglo-Saxons had any knowledge of the New Testament? I think not; we might now be arguing whether they got their knowledge of Cain and Abel from Christian or from Jewish missionaries. There is no mention of the great dogmas of Christianity — the Incarnation, the Crucifixion, the Resurrection, or the Salvation of Mankind. The name of Christ does not appear. It can scarcely be claimed that the tone of the poem is overwhelmingly Christian. Even the references to judgement after death might be explained as echoes of various Old Testament passages and the shooter of lines 1743–1746, with his bow and arrow, might be seen as a reference to Psalm xi. 2. Here too we may note William Whallon's recent claim that in *Beowulf* 'the words *fæder*, *alwalda*, and *metod* are as biblical as *pater*, *omnipotens*, and *fatum* are in the *Æneid*, and *Beowulf* is to this extent neither Christian nor un-Christian but pre-Christian'.

Of course, we have to admit that it was Christian missionaries who brought to Britain the story of Cain and Abel and the good news of the power of God and we probably have to agree that the great judgement referred to in lines 977–979 is not the Old Testament 'Day of the Lord'. Yet the absence of obvious Christian references remains a problem. It is, in my opinion, clear that we lack the evidence on which to base a definitive answer to the question 'How Christian is *Beowulf*?' We ought to recognize this — nothing emphasizes the truth of it more than the fantastic variety of theories about the meaning of *Beowulf*. The last word of the poem illustrates the dilemma. The Geatish warriors pay their final tribute to Beowulf thus:

> of all kings on earth
> he was the kindest, the most gentle,
> the most just to his people, the most eager for fame.

The last phrase translates the Old English word *lofgeornost*. As we have seen already, *lof* could have pagan or Christian connotations. For which *lof* was Beowulf eager? The pagan or the Christian? The answer to this is fundamental; here the divergence begins which produces such opposed views as those of Chadwick — 'however much coated over with Christian phraseology, the heroic poems were in reality of an essentially heathen character' — and of A. G. Brodeur — the 'pervasiveness [of the Christian passages], and the warmth and vigor of a number of them, show that the poet was a man of deep Christian conviction'. Another explanation of the difficulty under discussion is that of Kenneth Sisam 'that in this work the poet was not much concerned with Christianity and paganism'. Whether the *Beowulf* poet was hot, cold, or luke-warm, to the new faith is (I fear) still a matter of opinion.

8. *The Meaning of* Beowulf

As we embark on a brief examination of some of the theories which purport to explain *Beowulf*, we need to remind our-selves that some writers think that the poet was concerned only with telling a story. In the eyes of such people we are now dis-regarding the Anglo-Saxon equivalent of the Notice which Mark Twain prefixed to *The Adventures of Huckleberry Finn*:

Persons attempting to find a motive in this narrative will be prosecuted; persons attempting to find a moral in it will be banished; persons attempting to find a plot in it will be shot.

I think it unlikely that such a notice preceded *Beowulf*. That
many scholars agree is shown by the great number of motives
and morals which have been detected in it by those who
proceed from the assumption that *Beowulf* is the work of a
poet with a set purpose and not a stringing-together of old
pagan poems on a thread of Christian moralizing.

To some *Beowulf* is the work of a recently-converted pagan
who has assimilated the Old Testament to the Germanic code
rather than the Germanic code to the New Testament. Such
an assimilation would be a natural thing — both the Anglo-
Saxons and the Jews of the Old Testament were 'heroic'
peoples, warlike, with loyalties to comrade, tribe, and lord,
and with a love of jewels and precious metals. Old English
poets were much happier when telling the story of the book of
Exodus or of the Hebrew maiden Judith; the Germanic
warrior's armour sits uneasily on Christ's Apostles. 'In *Beowulf*
there is little that is distinctively Christian in the strict sense.
The words and conduct of the ideal characters are for the most
part designed to show qualities such as courage, loyalty,
generosity, and wisdom, which are admired by good men of
any creed. Other characteristics, such as determination to
exact vengeance, are not in accord with Christian doctrine, but
were probably still admired by the majority of Anglo-Saxons
in Christian times.' So Kenneth Sisam.

This lack of obvious Christian references has led some to
adopt an almost humanistic view of the poem, which they see
as glorifying 'man's unconquerable mind'. T. M. Gang seems
to come close to this: 'Perhaps it would not be excessively
rash to suggest that *Beowulf*, so far from being a Christianized
epic, is an attempt at a sort of secular Saints' life: the sort of
poem that would meet Alcuin's strictures on the heroic poetry
without altogether sacrificing the heroic stories to instruction.'

But many modern interpretations are specifically Christian.
The difficulty of reconciling such an interpretation with the
absence of obvious Christian references is brilliantly met by
J. R. R. Tolkien, who sees *Beowulf* as the work of a Christian
poet deliberately portraying ancient pre-Christian days and

emphasizing the nobility of the pagan Germanic world. According to this explanation, we have to do with the Christian interpretation of pagan myths expressed in a very special way, namely, through the evocation of the pagan world at its best; hence the world of *Beowulf* remains pagan, though viewed by a Christian poet. Charles Donahue has used Celtic sources to demonstrate the possibility that the poet chose Old Testament references alone because he was showing his ancestors as 'righteous heathens'. 'For our insular Christian poet,' he concludes, 'Christianity is latent in the Old Testament and the holy men depicted there are *Christi figurae*.'

Other critics have been less distressed by the poet's failure to mention the great dogmas of Christianity or the name of Christ. Thus Fr. Klaeber wrote: 'We might even feel inclined to recognize features of the Christian Savior in the destroyer of hellish fiends, the warrior brave and gentle, blameless in thought and deed, the king that dies for his people.' A. Campbell sees *Beowulf* as the creation of Anglo-Saxon monasticism; in his view 'the "Christian colouring" of *Beowulf* is now well understood to be an original and integral element in the poem'. M. B. McNamee has gone further and has produced an allegorical interpretation.

The Anglo-Saxon audience, he argues, had a taste for obscure allegory and riddles. To such an audience, all that was necessary was a clue sufficient to suggest the identification. *Beowulf* is an 'allegory of salvation'; the clue which suggests the identification of Beowulf and the Christian Saviour is (according to Father McNamee) the fact that Grendel and his mother are repeatedly described as inmates of Hell, powers of darkness, and so on. Thus the poet expresses the Christian message through the Anglo-Saxon myth. The fight with Grendel betokens the Salvation of Man, the fight with Grendel's mother Christ's Resurrection and the Harrowing of Hell, and the fight with the Dragon Christ's death. Such an interpretation is (I believe) possible granted that *Beowulf* is a sophisticated poem composed, perhaps by a monk, for a deeply Christian, perhaps monastic, audience well versed in the Latin Fathers. But the fact that allegory is elsewhere made explicit in Old English poetry argues against it, as does the lack of real Christian feeling.

Some recent writers have advanced the view that Beowulf is being criticized by the poet. One is Margaret E. Goldsmith: 'Beowulf... was written to present the quasi-historical Beowulf fighting in his youth as God's champion against the devilish brood of Cain and fighting in his old age against the Ancient Serpent who tempts all the sons of Adam to love power and wealth more than God.' For Mrs. Goldsmith, Beowulf was conducting a Holy War against evil and his final failure arose from his pride, his love of treasure, and his rejection of God's help. The poet, she believes, took the old story to illustrate a moral lesson — that only suffering and death can attend the search for earthly riches.

In my opinion, this is a misreading of the poem. I cannot agree that the poet portrays Beowulf as an arrogant and gold-seeking king deserted by God; I would argue that Beowulf did exactly what one would expect of an heroic king in the circumstances. It is true that Hrothgar's homily (lines 1724–1768) warns Beowulf against pride and greed. But it ends with the reminder that Beowulf too must die. It seems to me wrong to take the warning against pride and greed as the key to the poem without recognizing the importance of Hrothgar's final statement that death will come for Beowulf — as it must for all men and for all kings, good and bad. The poet is not necessarily implying that Beowulf neglected the warning and that pride and greed were the cause of his death. We are entitled to believe (if we wish) that he heeded Hrothgar's advice. We might call as evidence fifty years of good kingship, followed by death in the service of his people. Moreover, both Beowulf (lines 2794–2798) and Wiglaf (lines 2874–2876) state clearly that God gave him the victory. The fact that Beowulf dies is no reason for believing that he has been deserted by God or that he has done something wrong. That sinners live and saints die is a fact of everyday experience which does not prove that God is with the former and against the latter. Since life is transitory, death is no reproach. A man can but die on his death-day; neither Fate nor the Grace of God can do anything to keep alive the man who is doomed (*fǣ̇ġe*). Beowulf's death, like ours, is inevitable.

More plausible than this theory (it seems to me) is the suggestion that the poet was not entirely happy with Beowulf's handling of the dragon-fight. Views of this kind depend on taking the last word of the poem *lofġeornost* ('most eager for praise') as a word of criticism. 'He is saved from defeat,' says J. R. R. Tolkien, 'and the essential object, destruction of the dragon, only achieved by the loyalty of a subordinate. Beowulf's chivalry would otherwise have ended in his own useless death, with the dragon still at large.' Professor Tolkien detects the same fault in Byrhtnoth, the leader of the Anglo-Saxon army defeated by the Danes at the battle of Maldon in 991. It is in essence a failure to grow with one's obligations: Beowulf and Byrhtnoth were, according to this view, platoon-commanders in outlook, but army-commanders in responsibility.

This view has been taken up by later writers. Some think Beowulf is the 'one' referred to in Wiglaf's observation (lines 3077–3083):

Many thanes must often suffer
because of the will of one, as we do now.
We could not dissuade the king we loved,
or in any way restrain the lord of our land
from drawing his sword against the gold-warden,
from letting him lie where he had long lain
and remain in his lair until the world's end.

One claims that Beowulf 'makes hardly any preparations for the fight'. According to another, 'we may . . . say the fight against the dragon was against the interests of the country and detrimental to its defence'.*

But the poem does not read to me like a criticism of Beowulf. I cannot agree that the first two lines of Wiglaf's remark necessarily refer to Beowulf; the 'one' could have been the thief

---

* G. N. Garmonsway and N. F. Blake respectively.

who first plundered the hoard or the man who cursed the gold or even the dragon itself. It would surprise me if the implication of lines 3079–3083 is that Wiglaf or the poet really believed that the country would have been better off in the long run if Beowulf had stayed at home or really thought that Beowulf should have let the dragon lie. What streams of reproach would have fallen and would now be falling about his hapless head if he had followed that advice! Is one really to believe that Wiglaf meant that he should have? I doubt it. His remarks could be a hyperbolic expression of love for Beowulf — 'rather the dragon's ravages than Beowulf dead'. Such lines as these illustrate the danger of placing too much reliance on individual words or sentences in a poem like *Beowulf*, where the poet is sometimes more concerned with the effect of the moment than with complete internal consistency; see Appendix VD. Thus Beowulf's speech (lines 2532–2535):

> This is not your undertaking, nor is it
> possible for any man but me alone
> to pit his strength against the gruesome one,
> and perform great deeds,

has been taken to prove that he was guilty of arrogant and irresponsible reliance on his own strength. The passage need not mean this — after all Beowulf was the Geats' best warrior and 'boasting' in the sense of 'naming one's play', describing a great feat one intended to perform, was the accepted thing in heroic times. The suggestion that it does is contradicted, not only by passages like Wiglaf's comment (lines 2874–2876):

> yet God, Giver of Victories, granted
> that he should avenge himself with his sword
> single-handed, when all his courage was called for,

but also (it seems to me) by the overall impression of Beowulf's character one gets from the whole poem. The assertion that Beowulf took insufficient precautions is not supported by the facts. He prepared an iron shield and carried a sword and a knife. He took Wiglaf and ten other helpers — admittedly not an army, but enough if the ten had not run away. Was it

Beowulf's fault they did? Was it Beowulf's fault his sword broke? We need to remember that Beowulf was not immortal and that the misery which followed his death is no reason for despairing or for blaming Beowulf, but is merely part of the machinery of life. We are not bound to believe that the last word of the poem can be taken only as a lash of criticism. To me it seems clearly a word of praise.

An interesting variation on J. R. R. Tolkien's theory has recently been put forward by John Leyerle:

> The poem presents a criticism of the essential weakness of the society it portrays. Such criticism was D. H. Lawrence's criterion for greatness in literature. Heroic society inevitably encouraged a king to act the part of a hero, yet the heroic king, however glorious, was apt to be a mortal threat to his nation. An individual's desire for glory . . . becomes an increasingly dangerous motivation as a man's responsibility for leadership grows. Even without such a desire, a leader's excessive reliance on his personal strength easily brings calamity.

Here a sophisticated Christian poet is seen criticizing the code by which Beowulf lived rather than Beowulf himself. Such a Beowulf — youthful in outlook, overbold, living and dying according to his code — would still be worthy of the flood of tears, the splendid tomb, the treasures, the elaborate funeral rites, and the noble dirge, lavished upon him by the Geats. He is an altogether different person from the 'deluded old man' 'blinded by arrogance and desire for the treasure' presented by Mrs. Goldsmith.

Whether he is the Beowulf presented to us by the poet is arguable. E. G. Stanley too detects criticism of the code:

> I have said elsewhere that it seems to me that, though the poet presents the heroic ideal of his people lovingly, he presents it as ultimately unavailing and therefore not worth ambition. Perhaps there is a hint even that Beowulf, being a pagan too eager in the hour of his death for posthumous fame and the sight of gold — what else *can* pagans think about when they die? — will not, for all his virtues, be saved from everlasting damnation in hell. Once the modern reader feels that hint

he ceases to read the poem simply as the Germanic heroic ideal presented elegiacally. What is implied is that the poet is aware of the fact that the pagan heroic ideal stands in conflict with the ascetic ideal of Christianity, as it was known in the English monasteries of the poet's time. By the standards of that higher ideal the heroic ideal is insufficient.

If the poet saw this contrast so clearly (a contrast which certainly emerges in the story of King Sigbert of East Anglia told in section 7 above) and intended to bring it out, it seems strange that he did not do so more clearly; one would expect more than a 'hint'. This, I must admit, is a continuing riddle to me: if Old English poets such as the author of *Beowulf* were passionate Christians writing with a clear Christian purpose, why did they fail to make clear beyond peradventure the aim they had in view and the passion which they felt? One can see with Miss Whitelock that, once the poet had chosen as his theme the ravages of monsters among mankind, he would be led to the giants of Genesis and so might limit himself to Old Testament allusions. But this would not explain why he would choose that particular material to illustrate the deficiencies of the heroic code in comparison with Christianity. Might not Alcuin have said to him in his turn: 'What has Beowulf to do with Christ?'

Stanley goes on to admit that 'some readers will be reluctant to read the poem in that way'. I am among them. I am very doubtful whether the poet meant us to feel that 'hint'. He himself remarks of Beowulf (lines 2819–2820) that

> his soul migrated
> from his breast to meet the judgement of righteous men.

Wiglaf has no doubt about Beowulf's fate (lines 3107–3109):

> and then let us carry our king,
> the man we loved, to where he must
> long remain in the Lord's protection.

The final epitaph reads to me as a climax of praise, not an anti-climax of criticism:

they said that of all the kings on earth
he was the kindest, the most gentle,
the most just to his people, the most eager for fame.

When I close my copy of *Beowulf*, I find myself more in
sympathy with Kenneth Sisam's observation that the poem 'is a
"mirror" of noble conduct'. This is what I feel now. But this
too is no more than an opinion held by one twentieth-century
reader at one point in time as he reacts to the poem, and in the
end you too will have to adopt an interpretation which appeals
to you; you too will have to react to the poem.

9. *The Poetry*

In the words of Alan Bliss, 'Old English poetry is not at
all primitive; on the contrary, it is very highly artificial and
sophisticated.' The natural question 'In what ways?' can be
answered by a consideration of the metrical form, the vocabulary, and the poets' handling of certain themes and their response to certain situations.

In general, Old English poetry tends to fall into verse para-
graphs with enjambement between the lines and with frequent
repetition. The demands of alliteration make this repetition
necessary. In the hands of the feeble craftsman, of course, it is
often empty. But the good poet, by varying his point and by
giving additional information, is able to enrich his verse. A
simple illustration on a not particularly high level may help to
explain this.

In *The Battle of Maldon*, lines 113–115, we read:

> Wund wearð Wulfmær, wælræste ġecēas,
> Byrhtnōðes mæġ, hē mid billum wearð,
> his swustersunu, swīðe forhēawen.

Literally glossed this means

> Wounded became Wulfmær, rest among the slain chose,
> Byrhtnoth's kinsman, he with swords became,
> his sister's son, cruelly hewn down.

Here the first half-line tells the whole story in brief. The remaining first half-lines tell us who Wulfmær was — the kinsman of the English commander and (more important) his sister's son, which, as Tacitus pointed out, was a particularly important tie in Germanic society. The second half-lines all fill out the word 'wounded' — he was fatally wounded, he was wounded by swords, he was cruelly wounded. Here we see in simple form the technique of repetition with variation and advance.

Within the verse paragraph, the alliterative unit is the line. The alliteration falls on accented syllables. The first accented syllable of the second half-line ('the head-stave') gives the alliterating letter. Thus in the quotation above, line 113 alliterates on *w* (*wund . . .Wulf . . . wæl*; the unaccented *wearð* is not part of the scheme), line 114 on *b* (*Byrht . . . bill*), and line 115 on *sw*. The maximum number of alliterations in any one line is three (as in line 113). The minimum — naturally enough — is two, one in each half-line.

But the metrical unit is the half-line, and the metrical patterns were selected from those common in ordinary speech. A few examples will suffice to show the close relationship between verse rhythms and those of prose. One common pattern (known as type A) is 'stress unstress stress unstress'. The following are some of the combinations which often fall into that pattern:

adjective + noun (*lāðe ġystas* 'hateful strangers'),
subject + verb (*beornas fēollon* 'warriors fell'),
object + verb (*gāras bǣron* 'spears [they] carried'),
complement + verb (*ġearwe stōdon* 'ready stood'),
infinitive + verb (*wealdan mōston* 'to wield were able'),
and noun + adjective (*wīġes ġeorne* 'for war eager').

Again, *brimlīþendra* is the genitive plural of a present participle used as a noun 'of the seafarers'. By itself it makes up a half-line of the pattern Da described below.

There are six of these basic patterns and each half-line is an example or a variation of one of them. J. R. R. Tolkien has given us the following Modern English examples of the normal forms of these six patterns:

A	falling — falling	*knights in armour*
B	rising — rising	*the roaring sea*
C	clashing	*on high mountains*
Da	falling by stages	*bright archangels*
Db	broken fall	*bold brazenfaced*
E	fall and rise	*highcrested elms*

He goes on to observe:

These are the normal patterns of four elements into which Old English words naturally fell, and into which modern English words still fall. They can be found in any passage of prose, ancient or modern. Verse of this kind differs from prose, *not* in rearranging words to fit a special rhythm, repeated or varied in successive lines, but in choosing the simpler and more compact word-patterns and clearing away extraneous matter, so that these patterns stand opposed to one another.

Part of the artificiality of Old English poetry lay in the restricted number of patterns permitted. Part lay in the special poetic vocabulary, especially in the poetic compounds and in the number of archaic words retained for their alliterative value. Here should be noted the kenning, a sort of condensed metaphor in which (*a*) is compared to (*b*) without (*a*) or the point of the comparison being made explicit; the metaphor 'The camel is the ship of the desert' would become the kenning 'The desert ship lurched on.' Thus one Old English poet tells us of a ship out of control and driven by the storm in the words 'The sea-steed heeds not the bridle', while the *Exodus* poet speaks of minstrels as 'laughter-smiths'. An audience would require time to grasp the implications of such sophisticated 'riddling' comparisons; this and the fact that there seems to have been a harp accompaniment would suggest that Old English poetry was recited much more slowly than modern poetry.

Another important point about Old English poetry is that the formulae inherited from the days when the poetry was orally composed survive in the lettered poetry. These formulae are set metrical combinations which can be varied according to the needs of alliteration. Thus the phrase 'on the sea' can be expressed by *on hranrāde* 'on the whale-road' or by *on seġlrāde* 'on the sail-road', and a lord may be a *frēawine* 'lord-friend' or a *goldwine* 'gold-friend'. Similar variations exist for many other expressions, e.g. 'deprived of joys' (a phrase frequently used of an exile), the epic formula 'we have heard . . .', and the Christian concepts of God.

These formulae often cluster about a particular theme. Thus the exile — the man cut off from his *comitatus* — becomes a symbol of misery and the poets work the changes on phrases traditionally associated with this idea. Similarly the beasts of battle — the wolf, the raven, and the eagle — are to be found when a battle is imminent. Eager for carrion, they utter their grim howls and cries. Originally, they were doubtless a reality on the battlefield as they devoured the bodies of the slain; later their appearance is conventional and often, in the hands of the clumsy or uninspired poet, perfunctory. It is an interesting confirmation of the genius of the *Beowulf* poet that his is the most brilliant handling of this theme — not only in the detailed treatment, but also in the significant place it has in the overall structure of the poem; see lines 3021–3027. 'Here indeed,' Adrien Bonjour remarks, 'the beasts of battle are briefly turned into a symbol of the ultimate triumph of death, the common destiny of dynasties, and the final fate of man . . . — all leading to that crowning picture of calamity.'

I cannot do better here than quote the remarks of Alan Bliss:

The appreciation of Old English poetry cannot be learned in a day, but it can be learned without great difficulty, provided it is approached in the right spirit. The student must remember that, although Old English poetry resembles Modern English poetry in many ways, it is nevertheless very different from it. He must not expect to find a regularly recurring rhythm such as is found in Modern English until fairly recently; rather he must learn to recognize (and admire) the way in which the natural rhythms of English speech are organized into a poetic vehicle of immense power and flexibility, capable of achieving the most subtle and varied effects. Reading aloud is very helpful; if the proper stresses, quantities and pauses are observed, the poetic qualities will soon make themselves felt. The student of today, familiar as he is with various varieties of 'free verse', is probably better equipped to appreciate Old English poetry to the full than the student of any previous generation.

In doing so, you will find that alliterative verse is capable of varied and powerful effects, especially in the hands of a master-craftsman like the *Beowulf* poet.

In an attempt to demonstrate this, two passages from *Beowulf* are printed in Appendix II with a guide to pronunciation, a literal translation, and a brief commentary. Other passages which would repay study in the original include the description of Grendel's mere (lines 1357–1376), the father's lament for his dead son (lines 2444–2459), and the 'beasts of battle' passage already mentioned (lines 3021–3027). The poet's sense of atmosphere will emerge clearly from a study of these passages. A few other illustrations of this gift will not be out of place — the eagerness of Scyld's ice-covered funeral ship as it strains at the anchor on the ebb-tide (lines 32–33); the splendour of Heorot destined to be destroyed by fire (lines 81–85); the fleshiness of Grendel's greedy devouring of the Geat in Heorot (lines 739–745); the 'slaughter-stained' winter of uneasy truce at Finnesburh (lines 1127–1133); the renewed agony of Hrothgar when Grendel's mother makes her attack to avenge her son (lines 1322–1344); the fatal question which provokes the renewal of the Danish–Heathobard feud (lines 2047–2052).

Other aspects of the poet's artistry deserve mention. In the account of the fight between Beowulf and the dragon, he discards the element of suspense in its crudest form by telling us on several occasions the outcome of the struggle. Four times we learn that Beowulf is doomed (lines 2309 ff., 2341 ff., 2419 ff., and 2586 ff.); twice we learn that the dragon is doomed (lines 2323 and 2341 ff.). Yet there is still plenty to interest and excite not only the listening thanes but also a modern audience. A similar device is exploited in lines 702–738, where we are told three times that Grendel will lose the fight with Beowulf. Here there is tension throughout between Grendel's hopes (he does not know he must fail) and the truth

known to poet and audience. This tension explodes violently
at line 750. Grendel has had his gloating laugh, his meal of
human flesh. Suddenly Beowulf grasps him:

> Instantly that monster, hardened by crime,
> realized that never had he met any man
> in the regions of earth, in the whole world,
> with so strong a grip. He was seized with terror.

This passage is worth further comment. It falls naturally into
three divisions, each introduced by the word *cōm* 'come' —
lines 702–709, 710–719, and 720–738. Klaeber remarks 'Some
enthusiasts have found the threefold bell-like announcement of
Grendel's approach a highly dramatic device.' Within these
three divisions we find the same sequence — the monster, the
hall, the poet's comment that Grendel will fail, the waiting
Beowulf. We find the changing scenes brilliantly conveyed by
visual imagery. To make a film of this section would not be
difficult. The first outside shot would show a dim figure, a
sceaduġenga, a stalker in the shadows. Then we should see the
hall. In the next shot the dim figure has become Grendel and
he can now see the hall. In the next shot, he approaches the
hall and bursts in. He is a *rinc* 'a man' — something vaguely
human in shape. Between these outside shots we move into the
hall. In the last scene (as Alain Renoir has pointed out) the
screen would be dark except for Grendel's eyes, from which
there gleams a baleful light.

Inevitably some of the effect is lost in translation. Thus
Grendel is said to come *scrīpan* 'shrithing' (a rhyme with
'writhing'). This verb is used four times in *Beowulf*. In line
163, it is used of the mysterious creatures of hell, of whom
Grendel is one. In line 650, the shadowy shapes of darkness
came *scrīpan* dusky beneath the clouds. In line 703 (the passage
under discussion), it is used of one particular shadowy shape
which proves to be Grendel. In line 2569, the dragon, fiery
and twisted, came *scrīpan* towards Beowulf, hastening to battle.
To our poet, it is thus a word with sinister associations, one
which describes the movement of both Grendel and the dragon

— smooth, supple, graceful, sinewy, but full of menace, ready to explode instantly into attack. It is a pity we have lost the word; indeed, the translator has chosen to revive it.

10. Conclusion

I sincerely hope that what I have written here will not stand between you and the poem. I have tried to be mindful of Wilfrid Gibson's warning:

> 'Poetry should be *this* —
>   Not that!'
> 'Poetry should be *that* —
>   Not this!'
> The little critics hiss
> And contradict each other flat;
> While, careless of what poetry should be,
> The poet goes on writing poetry.

Both Kevin and I hope you will enjoy *Beowulf*, either because or in spite of us. Whether it leaves you with a feeling of despair or hope is a personal matter. Of course Beowulf's efforts were wasted in one sense: the Geats are no longer a great people. Similarly, since empires and civilizations rise and fall, the efforts of all great men in a sense come to nothing. This is true of little men too. Yet there is no need for despair:

> The souls of the righteous are in the hand of God,
> and there shall no torment touch them.

Today, in this nuclear age, with man's inhumanity to man daily more apparent on all levels and the powers of darkness in seeming ascendancy throughout the world, we may see *Beowulf* as a triumphant affirmation of the value of a good life: as the poet himself says,

> *Brūc ealles well*
> Make good use of everything.

Heathmont
Victoria
Australia
August 1967

BEOWULF

Listen!
      The fame of Danish kings
in days gone by, the daring feats
worked by those heroes are well known to us.
    Scyld Scefing* often deprived his enemies,
many tribes of men, of their mead-benches.
He terrified his foes; yet he, as a boy,
had been found a waif; fate made amends for that.
He prospered under heaven, won praise and honour,
until the men of every neighbouring tribe,
across the whale's way, were obliged to obey him
and pay him tribute. He was a noble king!
Then a son was born to him, a child
in the court, sent by God to comfort
the Danes; for He had seen their dire distress,
that once they suffered hardship for a long while,
lacking a lord; and the Lord of Life,
King of Heaven, granted this boy glory;
Beow was renowned — the name of Scyld's son
became known throughout the Norse lands.
By his own mettle, likewise by generous gifts
while he still enjoys his father's protection,
a young man must ensure that in later years
his companions will support him, serve
their prince in battle; a man who wins renown
will always prosper among any people.
    Then Scyld departed at the destined hour,
that powerful man sought the Lord's protection.
His own close companions carried him
down to the sea, as he, lord of the Danes,
had asked while he could still speak.
That well-loved man had ruled his land for many years.

* See Appendix VA.

32

There in harbour stood the ring-prowed ship,
the prince's vessel, icy, eager to sail;
and then they laid their dear lord,
the giver of rings, deep within the ship
by the mast in majesty; many treasures
and adornments from far and wide were gathered there.
I have never heard of a ship equipped
more handsomely with weapons and war-gear,
swords and corslets; on his breast
lay countless treasures that were to travel far
with him into the waves' domain.
They gave him great ornaments, gifts
no less magnificent than those men had given him
who long before had sent him alone,
child as he was, across the stretch of the seas.
Then high above his head they placed
a golden banner and let the waves bear him,
bequeathed him to the sea; their hearts were grieving,
their minds mourning. Mighty men
beneath the heavens, rulers in the hall,
cannot say who received that cargo.

When his royal father had travelled from the earth,
Beow of Denmark, a beloved king,
ruled long in the stronghold, famed
amongst men; in time Healfdene the brave
was born to him; who, so long as he lived,
grey-haired and redoubtable, ruled the noble Danes.
Beow's son Healfdene, leader of men,
was favoured by fortune with four children:
Heorogar and Hrothgar and Halga the good;
Yrse, the fourth, was Onela's queen,
the dear wife of that warlike Swedish king.

Hrothgar won honour in war,
glory in battle, and so ensured
his followers' support — young men
whose number multiplied into a mighty troop.
And he resolved to build a hall,

a large and noble feasting-hall
of whose splendours men would always speak,
and there to distribute as gifts to old and young
all the things that God had given him —
but not men's lives or the public land.
Then I heard that tribes without number, even
to the ends of the earth, were given orders
to decorate the hall. And in due course
(before very long) this greatest of halls
was completed. Hrothgar, whose very word was counted
far and wide as a command, called it Heorot.
He kept his promise, gave presents of rings
and treasure at the feasting. The hall towered high,
lofty and wide-gabled — fierce tongues of loathsome fire
had not yet attacked it, nor was the time yet near
when a mortal feud should flare between father-
and son-in-law, sparked off by deeds of deadly enmity.*

   Then the brutish demon who lived in darkness
impatiently endured a time of frustration:
day after day he heard the din of merry-making
inside the hall, and the sound of the harp
and the bard's clear song. He who could tell
of the origin of men from far-off times lifted his voice,
sang that the Almighty made the earth,
this radiant plain encompassed by oceans;
and that God, all powerful, ordained
sun and moon to shine for mankind,
adorned all regions of the world
with trees and leaves; and sang that He gave life
to every kind of creature that walks about earth.
So those warrior Danes lived joyful lives,
in complete harmony, until the hellish fiend
began to perpetrate base crimes.
This gruesome creature was called Grendel,
notorious prowler of the borderland, ranger of the moors,
the fen and the fastness; this cursed creature

* See Appendix Vb.

lived in a monster's lair for a time
after the Creator had condemned him
as one of the seed of Cain — the Everlasting Lord
avenged Abel's murder. Cain had
no satisfaction from that feud, but the Creator
sent him into exile, far from mankind,
because of his crime. He could no longer
approach the throne of grace, that precious place
in God's presence, nor did he feel God's love.
In him all evil-doers find their origin,
monsters and elves and spiteful spirits of the dead,
also the giants who grappled with God
for a long while; the Lord gave them their deserts.
     Then, under cover of night, Grendel came
to Hrothgar's lofty hall to see how the Ring-Danes
were disposed after drinking ale all evening;
and he found there a band of brave warriors,
well-feasted, fast asleep, dead to worldly sorrow,
man's sad destiny. At once that hellish monster,
grim and greedy, brutally cruel,
started forward and seized thirty thanes
even as they slept; and then, gloating
over his plunder, he hurried from the hall,
made for his lair with all those slain warriors.
Then at dawn, as day first broke,
Grendel's power was at once revealed;
a great lament was lifted, after the feast
an anguished cry at that daylight discovery.
The famous prince, best of all men, sat apart in mourning;
when he saw Grendel's gruesome footprints,
that great man grieved for his retainers.
This enmity was utterly one-sided, too repulsive,
too long-lasting. Nor were the Danes allowed respite,
but the very next day Grendel committed
violent assault, murders more atrocious than before,
and he had no qualms about it. He was caught up in his crimes.
Then it was not difficult to find the man

who preferred a more distant resting-place,
a bed in the outbuildings, for the hatred
of the hall-warden was quite unmistakable.
He who had escaped the clutches of the fiend
kept further off, at a safe distance.

Thus Grendel ruled, resisted justice,
one against all, until the best of halls
stood deserted. And so it remained:
for twelve long winters the lord of the Danes
was sorely afflicted with sorrows and cares;
then men were reminded in mournful songs
that the monster Grendel fought with Hrothgar
for a long time, fought with fierce hatred
committing crime and atrocity day after day
in continual strife. He had no wish for peace
with any of the Danes, would not desist
from his deadly malice or pay *wergild**—
No! None of the counsellors could hold out hope
Of handsome compensation at that slayer's hands.
But the cruel monster constantly terrified
young and old, the dark death-shadow
lurked in ambush; he prowled the misty moors
at the dead of night; men do not know
where such hell-whisperers shrithe in their wanderings.
Such were the many and outrageous injuries
that the fearful solitary, foe of all men,
endlessly inflicted; he occupied Heorot,
that hall adorned with treasures, on cloudless nights.
This caused the lord of the Danes deep,
heart-breaking grief. Strong men often sat

---

* The price set upon a man according to his rank which could be claimed
from the slayer by the kin of a man wrongfully killed. If it were not paid,
the death could be avenged by killing the slayer. Here Grendel's refusal to
pay emphasizes that he lives outside the law. In lines 2435 ff., Hrethel's
eldest son Herebeald has been killed by his own brother Hæthcyn. No
wergild can be paid. No vengeance is possible. Hrethel is therefore a helpless
mourner.

in consultation, trying in vain to devise
a good plan as to how best valiant men
could safeguard themselves against sudden attack.
At times they offered sacrifices to the idols
in their pagan tabernacles, and prayed aloud
to the soul-slayer that he would assist them
in their dire distress. Such was the custom
and comfort of the heathen; they brooded in their hearts
on hellish things — for the Creator, Almighty God,
the judge of all actions, was neglected by them;
truly they did not know how to praise the Protector of Heaven,
the glorious Ruler. Woe to the man who,
in his wickedness, commits his soul to the fire's embrace;
he must expect neither comfort nor change.
He will be damned for ever. Joy shall be his
who, when he dies, may stand before the Lord,
seek peace in the embrace of our Father.

Thus Healfdene's son endlessly brooded
over the afflictions of this time; that wise warrior
was altogether helpless, for the hardship upon them —
violent visitations, evil events in the night —
was too overwhelming, loathsome, and long-lasting.

One of Hygelac's thanes, Beowulf by name,
renowned among the Geats for his great bravery,
heard in his own country of Grendel's crimes;
he was the strongest man alive,
princely and powerful. He gave orders
that a good ship should be prepared, said he would sail
over the sea to assist the famous leader,
the warrior king, since he needed hardy men.
Wise men admired his spirit of adventure.
Dear to them though he was, they encouraged
the warrior and consulted the omens.
Beowulf searched out the bravest of the Geats,
asked them to go with him; that seasoned sailor
led fourteen thanes to the ship at the shore.

Days went by; the boat was on the water,

moored under the cliff. The warriors, all prepared,
stepped onto the prow — the water streams eddied,
stirred up sand; the men stowed
gleaming armour, noble war-gear
deep within the ship; then those warriors launched
the well-built boat and so began their journey.
Foaming at the prow and most like a sea-bird,
the boat sped over the waves, urged on by the wind;
until next day, at about the expected time,
so far had the curved prow come
that the travellers sighted land,
shining cliffs, steep hills,
broad headlands. So did they cross the sea;
their journey was at its end. Then the Geats
disembarked, lost no time in tying up
the boat — their corslets clanked;
the warriors gave thanks to God
for their safe passage over the sea.*
   Then, on the cliff-top, the Danish watchman
(whose duty it was to stand guard by the shore)
saw that the Geats carried flashing shields
and gleaming war-gear down the gangway,
and his mind was riddled with curiosity.
Then Hrothgar's thane leaped onto his horse
and, brandishing a spear, galloped
down to the shore; there, he asked at once:
'Warriors! Who are you, in your coats of mail,
who have steered your tall ship over the sea-lanes
to these shores? I've been a coastguard here
for many years, kept watch by the sea,
so that no enemy band should encroach
upon this Danish land and do us injury.
Never have warriors, carrying their shields,
come to this country in a more open manner.
Nor were you assured of my leaders' approval,
my kinsmen's consent. I've never set eyes

* The original of this passage is printed and discussed in Appendix IIB.

on a more noble man, a warrior in armour,
than one among your band; he's no mere retainer,
so ennobled by his weapons. May his looks never belie him,
and his lordly bearing. But now, before you step
one foot further on Danish land
like faithless spies, I must know
your lineage. Bold seafarers,
strangers from afar, mark my words
carefully: you would be best advised
quickly to tell me the cause of your coming.'
    The man of highest standing, leader of that troop,
unlocked his hoard of words, answered him:
'We are all Geats, hearth-companions of Hygelac;
my father was famed far and wide,
a noble lord, Ecgtheow by name —
he endured many winters before he,
in great old age, went on his way; every wise man
in this world readily recalls him.
We have sailed across the sea to seek your lord,
Healfdene's son, protector of the people,
with most honourable intentions; give us your guidance!
We have come on an errand of importance
to the great Danish prince; nor, I imagine, will the cause
of our coming long remain secret. You will know
whether it is true — as we have heard tell —
that here among the Danes a certain evil-doer,
a fearful solitary, on dark nights commits deeds
of unspeakable malice — damage
and slaughter. In good conscience
I can counsel Hrothgar, that wise and good man,
how he shall overcome the fiend,
and how his anguish shall be assuaged —
if indeed his fate ordains that these foul deeds
should ever end, and be avenged;
he will suffer endless hardship otherwise,
dire distress, as long as Heorot, best of dwellings,
stands unshaken in its lofty place.'

Still mounted, the coastguard,
a courageous thane, gave him this reply:
'The discriminating warrior — one whose mind is keen —
must perceive the difference between words and deeds.
But I see you are a company well disposed
towards the Danish prince. Proceed, and bring
your weapons and armour! I shall direct you.
And I will command my companions, moreover,
to guard your ship with honour
against any foe — your beached vessel,
caulked so recently — until the day that timbered craft
with its curved prow shall carry back
the beloved man across the sea currents
to the shores of the storm-loving Geats:
he who dares deeds with such audacity and valour
shall be granted safety in the squall of battle.'
    Then they hurried on. The ship lay still;
securely anchored, the spacious vessel
rode on its hawser. The boar crest, brightly gleaming,
stood over their helmets: superbly tempered,
plated with glowing gold, it guarded the lives
of those grim warriors. The thanes made haste,
marched along together until they could discern
the glorious, timbered hall, adorned with gold;
they saw there the best-known building
under heaven. The ruler lived in it;
its brilliance carried across countless lands.
Then the fearless watchman pointed out the path
leading to Heorot, bright home of brave men,
so that they should not miss the way;
that bold warrior turned his horse, then said:
'I must leave you here. May the Almighty Father,
of His grace, guard you in your enterprise.
I will go back to the sea again,
and there stand watch against marauding bands.'
    The road was paved; it showed those warriors
the way. Their corslets were gleaming,

the strong links of shining chain-mail
clinked together. When the sea-stained travellers
had reached the hall itself in their fearsome armour,
they placed their broad shields
(worked so skilfully) against Heorot's wall.
Then they sat on a bench; the brave men's
armour sang. The seafarers' gear
stood all together, a grey-tipped forest
of ash spears; that armed troop was well equipped
with weapons.
     Then Wulfgar, a proud warrior,
asked the Geats about their ancestry:
'Where have you come from with these gold-plated shields,
these grey coats of mail, these visored helmets,
and this pile of spears? I am Hrothgar's
messenger, his herald. I have never seen
so large a band of strangers of such bold bearing.
You must have come to Hrothgar's court
not as exiles, but from audacity and high ambition.'
Then he who feared no man, the proud leader
of the Geats, stern-faced beneath his helmet,
gave him this reply: 'We are Hygelac's
companions at the bench: my name is Beowulf.
I wish to explain to Healfdene's son,
the famous prince, your lord,
why we have come if he, in his goodness,
will give us leave to speak with him.'
Wulfgar replied — a prince of the Vandals,
his mettle, his wisdom and prowess in battle
were widely recognized: 'I will ask
the lord of the Danes, ruler of the Scyldings,
renowned prince and ring-giver,
just as you request, regarding your journey,
and bring back to you at once whatever answer
that gracious man thinks fit to give me.'
  Then Wulfgar hurried to the place where Hrothgar sat,
grizzled and old, surrounded by his thanes;

the brave man moved forward until he stood
immediately before the Danish lord;
he well knew the customs of warriors.
Wulfgar addressed his friend and leader:
'Geatish men have travelled to this land,
come from far, across the stretch of the seas.
These warriors call their leader Beowulf;
they ask, my lord, that they should be allowed
to speak with you. Gracious Hrothgar,
do not give them *no* for answer.
They, in their armour, seem altogether worthy
of the highest esteem. I have no doubt of their leader's
might, he who has brought these brave men to Heorot.'
Hrothgar, defender of the Danes, answered:
'I knew him when he was a boy;
his illustrious father was called Ecgtheow;
Hrethel the Geat gave him his only daughter
in marriage; now his son, with daring spirit,
has voyaged here to visit a loyal friend.
And moreover, I have heard seafarers say —
men who have carried rich gifts to the Geats
as a mark of my esteem — that in the grasp
of his hand that man renowned in battle
has the might of thirty men. I am convinced
that Holy God, of His great mercy,
has directed him to us West-Danes★
and that he means to come to grips with Grendel.
I will reward this brave man with treasures.
Hurry! Tell them to come in and meet
our band of kinsmen; and make it clear, too,
that they are most welcome to the Danes!'
Then Wulfgar went to the hall door with Hrothgar's reply:
'My conquering lord, the leader of the East-Danes★

★ The contradiction between East-Danes and West-Danes is only
apparent. For alliterative convenience the poet at various times refers to
Hrothgar's people — the Danes or Scyldings — as North-, South-, East-,
and West-Danes, and also as Bright-, Ring-, and Spear-Danes.

commands me to tell you that he knows your lineage
and that you, so bold in mind, are welcome
to these shores from over the rolling sea.
You may see Hrothgar in your armour,
under your helmets, just as you are;
but leave your shields out here, and your deadly ashen spears,
let them await the outcome of your words.'
    Then noble Beowulf rose from the bench,
flanked by his fearless followers; some stayed behind
at the brave man's bidding, to stand guard over their armour.
Guided by Wulfgar, the rest hurried into Heorot
together; there went that hardy man, stern-faced
beneath his helmet, until he was standing under Heorot's roof.
Beowulf spoke — his corslet, cunningly linked
by the smith, was shining: 'Greetings, Hrothgar!
I am Hygelac's kinsman and retainer. In my youth
I achieved many daring exploits. Word of Grendel's deeds
has come to me in my own country;
seafarers say that this hall Heorot,
best of all buildings, stands empty and useless
as soon as the evening light is hidden under the sky.
So, Lord Hrothgar, men known by my people
to be noble and wise advised me to visit you
because they knew of my great strength:
they saw me themselves when, stained by my enemies' blood,
I returned from the fight when I destroyed five,
a family of giants, and by night slew monsters
on the waves; I suffered great hardship,
avenged the affliction of the Storm-Geats and crushed
their fierce foes — they were asking for trouble.
And now, I shall crush the giant Grendel
in single combat. Lord of the mighty Danes,
guardian of the Scyldings, I ask one favour:
protector of warriors, lord beloved of your people,
now that I have sailed here from so far,
do not refuse my request — that I alone, with my band
of brave retainers, may cleanse Heorot.

I have also heard men say this monster
is so reckless he spurns the use of weapons.
Therefore (so that Hygelac, my lord,
may rest content over my conduct) I deny myself
the use of a sword and a broad yellow shield
in battle; but I shall grapple with this fiend
hand to hand; we shall fight for our lives,
foe against foe; and he whom death takes off
must resign himself to the judgement of God.
I know that Grendel, should he overcome me,
will without dread devour many Geats,
matchless warriors, in the battle-hall,
as he has often devoured Danes before. If death claims me
you will not have to cover my head,
for he already will have done so —
with a sheet of shining blood; he will carry off
the blood-stained corpse, meaning to savour it;
the solitary one will eat without sorrow
and stain his lair; no longer then
will you have to worry about burying my body.
But if battle should claim me, send this most excellent
coat of mail to Hygelac, this best of corslets
that protects my breast; it once belonged to Hrethel,
the work of Weland. Fate goes ever as it must!'
   Hrothgar, protector of the Scyldings, replied:
'Beowulf, my friend! So you have come here,
because of past favours, to fight on our behalf!
Your father Ecgtheow, by striking a blow,
began the greatest of feuds. He slew Heatholaf of the Wylfings
with his own hand; after that, the Geats
dared not harbour him for fear of war.
So he sailed here, over the rolling waves,
to this land of the South-Danes, the honoured Scyldings;
I was young then, had just begun to reign
over the Danes in this glorious kingdom,
this treasure-stronghold of heroes; my elder brother,
Heorogar, Healfdene's son, had died

not long before; he was a better man than I!
I settled your father's feud by payment;
I sent ancient treasures to the Wylfings
over the water's back; and Ecgtheow swore oaths to me.
It fills me with anguish to admit to all the evil
that Grendel, goaded on by his hatred,
has wreaked in Heorot with his sudden attacks
and infliction of injuries; my hall-troop is depleted,
my band of warriors; fate has swept them
into Grendel's ghastly clutches. Yet God can easily
prevent this reckless ravager from committing such crimes.
After quaffing beer, brave warriors of mine
have often boasted over the ale-cup
that they would wait in Heorot
and fight against Grendel with their fearsome swords.
Then, the next morning, when day dawned,
men could see that this great mead-hall was stained
by blood, that the floor by the benches
was spattered with gore; I had fewer followers,
dear warriors, for death had taken them off.
But first, sit down at our feast, and in due course,
as your inclination takes you, tell how warriors
have achieved greatness.'
                    Then, in the feasting-hall,
a bench was cleared for the Geats all together,
and there those brave men went and sat,
delighting in their strength; a thane did his duty —
held between his hands the adorned ale-cup,
poured out gleaming liquor; now and then the poet
raised his voice, resonant in Heorot; the warriors caroused,
no small company of Scyldings and Geats.
Ecglaf's son, Unferth, who sat at the feet
of the lord of the Scyldings, unlocked his thoughts
with these unfriendly words — for the journey of Beowulf,
the brave seafarer, much displeased him
in that he was unwilling for any man
in this wide world to gain more glory than himself:

'Are you the Beowulf who competed with Breca,
vied with him at swimming in the open sea
when, swollen with vanity, you both braved
the waves, risked your lives on deep waters
because of a foolish boast? No one,
neither friend nor foe, could keep you
from your sad journey, when you swam out to sea,
clasped in your arms the water-streams,
passed over the sea-paths, swiftly moved your hands
and sped over the ocean. The sea heaved,
the winter flood; for seven nights
you both toiled in the water; but Breca outstayed you,
he was the stronger; and then, on the eighth morning,
the sea washed him up on the shores of the Heathoreams.
From there he sought his own country,
the land of the Brondings who loved him well;
he went to his fair stronghold where he had a hall
and followers and treasures. In truth, Beanstan's son
fulfilled his boast that he could swim better than you.
So I am sure you will pay a heavy price —
although you have survived countless battle storms,
savage sword-play — if you dare
ambush Grendel in the watches of the night.'
Beowulf, the son of Ecgtheow, replied:
'Truly, Unferth my friend, all this beer
has made you talkative: you have told us much
about Breca and his exploits. But I maintain
I showed the greater stamina, endured
hardship without equal in the heaving water.
Some years ago when we were young men,
still in our youth, Breca and I made a boast,
a solemn vow, to venture our lives
on the open sea; and we kept our word.
When we swam through the water, we each held
a naked sword with which to ward off
whales; by no means could Breca
swim faster than I, pull away from me

through the press of the waves —
I had no wish to be separated from him.
So for five nights we stayed together in the sea,
until the tides tore us apart,
the foaming water, the freezing cold,
day darkening into night — until the north wind,
that savage warrior, rounded against us.
Rough were the waves; fishes in the sea
were roused to great anger. Then my coat of mail,
hard and hand-linked, guarded me against my enemies;
the woven war-garment, adorned with gold,
covered my breast. A cruel ravager
dragged me down to the sea-bed, a fierce monster
held me tightly in its grasp; but it was given to me
to bury my sword, my battle weapon,
in its breast; the mighty sea-beast
was slain by my blow in the storm of battle.
In this manner, and many times, loathsome monsters
harassed me fiercely; with my fine sword
I served them fittingly.
I did not allow those evil destroyers to enjoy
a feast, to eat me limb by limb
seated at a banquet on the sea-bottom;
but the next morning they lay in the sand
along the shore, wounded by sword strokes,
slain by battle-blades, and from that day on
they could not hinder seafarers from sailing
over deep waters. Light came from the east,
God's bright beacon; the swell subsided,
and I saw then great headlands,
cliffs swept by the wind. Fate will often spare
an undoomed man, if his courage is good.
As it was I slew nine sea-beasts
with my sword. I have never heard
of a fiercer fight by night under heaven's vault
nor of a man who endured more on the ocean streams.
But I escaped with my life from the enemies' clutches,

worn out by my venture. Then the swift current,
the surging water, carried me
to the land of the Lapps. I have not heard tell
that you have taken part in any such contests,
in the peril of sword-play. Neither you nor Breca
have yet dared such a deed with shining sword
in battle — I do not boast because of this —
though of course it is true you slew your own brothers,
your own close kinsmen. For that deed, however clever
you may be, you will suffer damnation in hell.
I tell you truly, son of Ecglaf,
that if you were in fact as unflinching
as you claim, the fearsome monster Grendel
would never have committed so many crimes
against your lord, nor created such havoc in Heorot;
but he has found he need not fear unduly
your people's enmity, fearsome assault
with swords by the victorious Scyldings.
So he spares none but takes his toll
of the Danish people, does as he will,
kills and destroys, expects no fight
from the Spear-Danes. But soon, quite soon,
I shall show him the strength, the spirit and skill
of the Geats. And thereafter, when day dawns,
when the radiant sun shines from the south
over the sons of men, he who so wishes
may enter the mead-hall without terror.'

Then the grizzled warrior, giver of gold,
was filled with joy; the lord of the Danes,
shepherd of his people, listened to Beowulf's
brave resolution and relied on his help.
The warriors laughed, there was a hum
of contentment. Wealhtheow came forward,
mindful of ceremonial — she was Hrothgar's queen;
adorned with gold, that proud woman
greeted the men in the hall, then offered the cup

to the Danish king first of all.
She begged him, beloved of his people,
to enjoy the feast; the king, famed
for victory, ate and drank in happiness.
Then the lady of the Helmings walked about the hall,
offering the precious, ornamented cup
to old and young alike, until at last
the queen, excellent in mind, adorned with rings,
moved with the mead-cup towards Beowulf.
She welcomed the Geatish prince and with wise words
thanked God that her wish was granted
that she might depend on some warrior for help
against such attacks. The courageous man
took the cup from Wealhtheow's hands
and, eager for battle, made a speech:
Beowulf, the son of Ecgtheow, said:
'When I put to sea, sailed
through the breakers with my band of men,
I resolved to fulfil the desire
of your people, or suffer the pangs of death,
caught fast in Grendel's clutches.
Here, in Heorot, I shall either work a deed
of great daring, or lay down my life.'
Beowulf's brave boast delighted Wealhtheow:
adorned with gold, the noble Danish queen
went to sit beside her lord.
    Then again, as of old, fine words were spoken
in the hall, the company rejoiced,
a conquering people, until in due course
the son of Healfdene wanted to retire
and take his rest. He realized the monster
meant to attack Heorot after the blue hour,
when black night has settled over all —
when shadowy shapes come shrithing
dark beneath the clouds. All the company rose.
Then the heroes Hrothgar and Beowulf saluted
one another; Hrothgar wished him luck

and control of Heorot, and confessed:
'Never since I could lift hand and shield,
have I entrusted this glorious Danish hall
to any man as I do now to you.
Take and guard this greatest of halls.
Make known your strength, remember your might,
stand watch against your enemy. You shall have
all you desire if you survive this enterprise.'
  Then Hrothgar, defender of the Danes,
withdrew from the hall with his band of warriors.
The warlike leader wanted to sleep with Wealhtheow,
his queen. It was said the mighty king
had appointed a hall-guard — a man who undertook
a dangerous duty for the Danish king,
elected to stand watch against the monster.
Truly, the leader of the Geats fervently trusted
in his own great strength and in God's grace.
Then he took off his helmet and his corslet
of iron, and gave them to his servant,
with his superb, adorned sword,
telling him to guard them carefully.
And then, before he went to his bed,
the brave Geat, Beowulf, made his boast:
'I count myself no less active in battle,
no less brave than Grendel himself:
thus, I will not send him to sleep with my sword,
so deprive him of life, though certainly I could.
Despite his fame for deadly deeds,
he is ignorant of these noble arts, that he might strike
at me, and hew my shield; but we, this night,
shall forego the use of weapons, if he dares fight
without them; and then may wise God,
the holy Lord, give glory in battle
to whichever of us He should think fitting.'
Then the brave prince leaned back, put his head
on the pillow while, around him,
many a proud seafarer lay back on his bed.

Not one of them believed he would see
day dawn, or ever return to his family
and friends, and the place where he was born;
they well knew that in recent days
far too many Danish men had come to bloody ends
in that hall. But the Lord wove the webs of destiny,
gave the Geats success in their struggle,
help and support, in such a way
that all were enabled to overcome their enemy
through the strength of one man. We cannot doubt
that mighty God has always ruled
over mankind.
                    Then the night prowler
came shrithing through the shadows. All the Geats
guarding Heorot had fallen asleep —
all except one. Men well knew that the evil enemy
could not drag them down into the shadows
when it was against the Creator's wishes,
but Beowulf, watching grimly for his adversary Grendel,
awaited the ordeal with increasing anger.
Then, under night's shroud, Grendel walked down
from the moors; he shouldered God's anger.
The evil plunderer intended to ensnare
one of the race of men in the high hall.
He strode under the skies, until he stood
before the feasting-hall, in front of the gift-building
gleaming with gold. And this night was not the first
on which he had so honoured Hrothgar's home.
But never in his life did he find hall-wardens
more greatly to his detriment. Then the joyless warrior
journeyed to Heorot. The outer door, bolted
with iron bands, burst open at a touch from his hands:
with evil in his mind, and overriding anger,
Grendel swung open the hall's mouth itself. At once,
seething with fury, the fiend stepped onto
the tessellated floor; a horrible light,
like a lurid flame, flickered in his eyes.

He saw many men, a group of warriors,
a knot of kinsmen, sleeping in the hall.
His spirits leapt, his heart laughed;
the savage monster planned to sever,
before daybreak, the life of every warrior
from his body — he fully expected to eat
his fill at the feast. But after that night
fate decreed that he should no longer feed off
human flesh. Hygelac's kinsman,
the mighty man, watched the wicked ravager
to see how he would make his sudden attacks.
The monster was not disposed to delay;
but, for a start, he hungrily seized
a sleeping warrior, greedily wrenched him,
bit into his body, drank the blood
from his veins, devoured huge pieces;
until, in no time, he had swallowed the whole man,
even his feet and hands. Now Grendel stepped forward,
nearer and nearer, made to grasp the valiant Geat
stretched out on his bed — the fiend reached towards him
with his open hand; at once Beowulf perceived
his evil plan, sat up and stayed Grendel's outstretched arm.
Instantly that monster, hardened by crime,
realized that never had he met any man
in the regions of earth, in the whole world,
with so strong a grip. He was seized with terror.
But, for all that, he was unable to break away.
He was eager to escape to his lair, seek the company
of devils, but he was restrained as never before.
Then Hygelac's brave kinsman bore in mind
his boast: he rose from the bed and gripped
Grendel fiercely. The fiend tried to break free,
his fingers were bursting. Beowulf kept with him.
The evil giant was desperate to escape,
if indeed he could, and head for his lair
in the fens; he could feel his fingers cracking
in his adversary's grip; that was a bitter journey

that Grendel made to the ring-hall Heorot.
The great room boomed; all the proud warriors —
each and every Dane living in the stronghold —
were stricken with panic. The two hall-wardens
were enraged. The building rang with their blows.
It was a wonder the wine-hall withstood
two so fierce in battle, that the fair building
did not fall to earth; but it stood firm,
braced inside and out with hammered
iron bands. I have heard tell that there,
where they fought, many a mead-bench,
studded with gold, started from the floor.
Until that time, elders of the Scyldings
were of the opinion that no man could wreck
the great hall Heorot, adorned with horns,
nor by any means destroy it unless it were gutted
by greedy tongues of flame. Again and again
clang and clatter shattered the night's silence;
dread numbed the North-Danes, seized all
who heard the shrieking from the wall,
the enemy of God's grisly lay of terror,
his song of defeat, heard hell's captive
keening over his wound. Beowulf held him fast,
he who was the strongest of all men
ever to have seen the light of life on earth.
By no means did the defender of thanes
allow the murderous caller to escape with his life;
he reckoned that the rest of Grendel's days
were useless to anyone. Then, time and again,
Beowulf's band brandished their ancestral swords;
they longed to save the life, if they
so could, of their lord, the mighty leader.
When they did battle on Beowulf's behalf,
struck at the monster from every side,
eager for his end, those courageous warriors
were unaware that no war-sword,
not even the finest iron on earth,

could wound their evil enemy,
for he had woven a secret spell
against every kind of weapon, every battle blade.
Grendel's death, his departure from this world,
was destined to be wretched, his migrating spirit
was fated to travel far into the power of fiends.
Then he who for years had committed crimes
against mankind, murderous in mind,
and had warred with God, discovered
that the strength of his body could not save him,
that Hygelac's brave kinsman held his hand
in a vice-like grip; each was a mortal enemy
to the other. The horrible monster
suffered grievous pain; a gaping wound
opened on his shoulder; the sinews sprang apart,
the muscles were bursting. Glory in battle
was given to Beowulf; fatally wounded,
Grendel was obliged to make for the marshes,
head for his joyless lair. He was
well aware that his life's days were done,
come to an end. After that deadly encounter
the desire of every Dane was at last accomplished.
    In this way did the wise and fearless man
who had travelled from far cleanse Hrothgar's hall,
release it from affliction. He rejoiced in his night's work,
his glorious achievement. The leader of the Geats
made good his boast to the East-Danes;
he had removed the cause of their distress,
put an end to the sorrow every Dane had shared,
the bitter grief that they had been constrained
to suffer. When Beowulf, brave in battle,
placed hand, arm and shoulder — Grendel's
entire grasp — under Heorot's spacious roof,
that was evidence enough of victory.
    Then I have heard that next morning
many warriors gathered round the gift-hall;

leaders of men came from every region,
from remote parts, to look on the wonder,
the tracks of the monster. Grendel's death
seemed no grievous loss to any of the men
who set eyes on the spoor of the defeated one,
saw how he, weary in spirit, overcome in combat,
fated and put to flight, had made for the lake
of water-demons — leaving tracks of life-blood.

There the water boiled because of the blood;
the fearful swirling waves reared up,
mingled with hot blood, battle gore;
fated, he hid himself, then joyless
laid aside his life, his heathen spirit,
in the fen lair; hell received him there.

After this, the old retainers left the lake
and so did the company of young men too;
brave warriors rode back on their gleaming horses
from this joyful journey. Then Beowulf's exploit
was acclaimed; many a man asserted
time and again that there was no better
shield-bearer in the whole world, to north or south
between the two seas, under the sky's expanse,
no man more worthy of his own kingdom.
Yet they found no fault at all with their friendly lord,
gracious Hrothgar — he was a great king.

At times the brave warriors spurred their bays,
horses renowned for their speed and stamina,
and raced each other where the track was suitable.
And now and then one of Hrothgar's thanes
who brimmed with poetry, and remembered lays,
a man acquainted with ancient traditions
of every kind, composed a new song
in correct metre. Most skilfully that man
began to sing of Beowulf's feat,
to weave words together, and fluently
to tell a fitting tale.
                    He recounted all he knew

of Sigemund, the son of Wæls;* many a strange story
about his exploits, his endurance, and his journeys
to earth's ends; many an episode
unknown or half-known to the sons of men, songs
of feud and treachery. Only Fitela knew of these things,
had heard them from Sigemund who liked to talk
of this and that, for he and his nephew
had been companions in countless battles —
they slew many monsters with their swords.
After his death, no little fame attached to Sigemund's name,
when the courageous man had killed the dragon,
guardian of the hoard. Under the grey rock
the son of the prince braved that dangerous deed
alone; Fitela was not with him;
for all that, as fate had it, he impaled
the wondrous serpent, pinned it to the rock face
with his patterned sword; the dragon was slain.
Through his own bravery, that warrior ensured
that he could enjoy the treasure hoard
at will; the son of Wæls loaded it all
onto a boat, stowed the shining treasure
into the ship; the serpent burned in its own flames.
Because of all his exploits, Sigemund,
guardian of strong men, was the best known
warrior in the world — so greatly had he prospered —
after Heremod's prowess, strength and daring
had been brought to an end, when, battling with giants,
he fell into the power of fiends, and was at once
done to death.† He had long endured
surging sorrows, had become a source
of grief to his people, and to all his retainers.
And indeed, in those times now almost forgotten,
many wise men often mourned that great warrior,
for they had looked to him to remedy their miseries;
they thought that the prince's son would prosper
and attain his father's rank, would protect his people,

* See Appendix Vc.　　　　　　　† See Appendix Vd.

their heirlooms and their citadel, the heroes' kingdom,
land of the Scyldings. Beowulf, Hygelac's kinsman,
was much loved by all who knew him,
by his friends; but Heremod was stained by sin.

    Now and then the brave men raced their horses,
ate up the sandy tracks — and they were so absorbed
that the hours passed easily. Stout-hearted warriors
without number travelled to the high hall
to inspect that wonder; the king himself, too,
glorious Hrothgar, guardian of ring-hoards,
came from his quarters with a great company, escorted
his queen and her retinue of maidens into the mead-hall.
Hrothgar spoke — he approached Heorot,
stood on the steps, stared at the high roof
adorned with gold, and at Grendel's hand:
'Let us give thanks at once to God Almighty
for this sight. I have undergone many afflictions,
grievous outrages at Grendel's hands; but God,
Guardian of heaven, can work wonder upon wonder.
Until now, I had been resigned,
had no longer believed that my afflictions
would ever end: this finest of buildings
stood stained with battle blood,
a source of sorrow to my counsellors;
they all despaired of regaining this hall
for many years to come, of guarding it from foes,
from devils and demons. Yet now one warrior
alone, through the Almighty's power, has succeeded
where we failed for all our fine plans.
Indeed, if she is still alive,
that woman (whoever she was) who gave birth
to such a son, to be one of humankind,
may claim that the Creator was gracious to her
in her child-bearing. Now, Beowulf,
best of men, I will love you in my heart
like a son; keep to our new kinship
from this day on. You shall lack

no earthly riches I can offer you.
Most often I have honoured a man for less,
given treasure to a poorer warrior,
more sluggish in the fight. Through your deeds
you have ensured that your glorious name
will endure for ever. May the Almighty grant you
good fortune, as He has always done before!'
    Beowulf, the son of Ecgtheow, answered:
'We performed that dangerous deed
with good will; at peril we pitted ourselves
against the unknown. I wish so much
that you could have seen him for yourself,
that fiend in his trappings, in the throes of death.
I meant to throttle him on that bed of slaughter
as swiftly as possible, with savage grips,
to hear death rattle in his throat
because of my grasp, unless he should escape me.
But I could not detain him, the Lord
did not ordain it — I did not hold my deadly enemy
firm enough for that; the fiend jerked free
with immense power. Yet, so as to save
his life, he left behind his hand,
his arm and shoulder; but the wretched monster
has bought himself scant respite;
the evil marauder, tortured by his sins,
will not live the longer, but agony
embraces him in its deadly bonds,
squeezes life out of his lungs; and now this creature,
stained with crime, must await the day of judgement
and his just deserts from the glorious Creator.'
    After this, the son of Ecglaf boasted less
about his prowess in battle — when all the warriors,
through Beowulf's might, had been enabled
to examine that hand, the fiend's fingers,
nailed up on the gables. Seen from in front,
each nail, each claw of that warlike,
heathen monster looked like steel —

a terrifying spike. Everyone said
that no weapon whatsoever, no proven sword
could possibly harm it, could damage
that battle-hardened, blood-stained hand.

   Then orders were quickly given for the inside of Heorot
to be decorated; many servants, both men and women,
bustled about that wine-hall, adorned that building
of retainers. Tapestries, worked in gold,
glittered on the walls, many a fine sight
for those who have eyes to see such things.
That beautiful building, braced within
by iron bands, was badly damaged;
the door's hinges were wrenched; when the monster,
damned by all his crimes, turned in flight,
despairing of his life, the hall roof only
remained untouched. Death is not easy
to escape, let him who will attempt it.
Man must go to the grave that awaits him —
fate has ordained this for all who have souls,
children of men, earth's inhabitants —
and his body, rigid on its clay bed,
will sleep there after the banquet.
                     Then it was time
for Healfdene's son to proceed to the hall,
the king himself was eager to attend the feast.
I have never heard of a greater band of kinsmen
gathered with such dignity around their ring-giver.
Then the glorious warriors sat on the benches,
rejoicing in the feast. Courteously
their kinsmen, Hrothgar and Hrothulf,
quaffed many a mead-cup, confident warriors
in the high hall. Heorot was packed
with feasters who were friends; the time was not yet come
when the Scyldings practised wrongful deeds.
Then Hrothgar gave Beowulf Healfdene's sword,
and a battle banner, woven with gold,
and a helmet and a corslet, as rewards for victory;

many men watched while the priceless, renowned sword
was presented to the hero. Beowulf emptied
the ale-cup in the hall; he had no cause
to be ashamed at those precious gifts.
There are few men, as far as I have heard,
who have given four such treasures, gleaming with gold,
to another on the mead-bench with equal generosity.
A jutting ridge, wound about with metal wires,
ran over the helmet's crown, protecting the skull,
so that well-ground swords, proven in battle,
could not injure the well-shielded warrior
when he advanced against his foes.
Then the guardian of thanes ordered
that eight horses with gold-plated bridles
be led into the courtyard; onto one was strapped
a saddle, inlaid with jewels, skilfully made.
That was the war-seat of the great king,
Healfdene's son, whenever he wanted
to join in the sword-play. That famous man
never lacked bravery at the front in battle,
when men about him were cut down like corn.
Then the king of the Danes, Ing's descendants,
presented the horses and weapons to Beowulf,
bade him use them well and enjoy them.
Thus the renowned prince, the retainers' gold-warden,
rewarded those fierce sallies in full measure,
with horses and treasure, so that no man
would ever find reason to reproach him fairly.
Furthermore, the guardian of warriors gave
a treasure, an heirloom at the mead-bench,
to each of those men who had crossed the sea
with Beowulf; and he ordered that gold
be paid for that warrior Grendel slew
so wickedly — as he would have slain many another,
had not foreseeing God and the warrior's courage
together forestalled him. The Creator ruled over
all humankind, even as He does today.

Wherefore a wise man will value forethought
and understanding. Whoever lives long
on earth, endures the unrest of these times,
will be involved in much good and much evil.
   Then Hrothgar, leader in battle, was entertained
with music — harp and voice in harmony.
The strings were plucked, many a song rehearsed,
when it was the turn of Hrothgar's poet
to please men at the mead-bench, perform in the hall.
He sang of Finn's troop, victims of surprise attack,
and of how that Danish hero, Hnæf of the Scyldings,
was destined to die among the Frisian slain.*
   Hildeburh, indeed, could hardly recommend
the honour of the Jutes; that innocent woman
lost her loved ones, son and brother,
in the shield-play; they fell, as fate ordained,
stricken by spears; and she was stricken with grief.
Not without cause did Hoc's daughter
mourn the shaft of fate, for in the light of morning
she saw that her kin lay slain under the sky,
the men who had been her endless pride
and joy. That encounter laid claim
to all but a few of Finn's thanes,
and he was unable to finish that fight
with Hnæf's retainer, with Hengest in the hall,
unable to dislodge the miserable survivors;
indeed, terms for a truce were agreed:
that Finn should give up to them another hall,
with its high seat, in its entirety,
which the Danes should own in common with the Jutes;
and that at the treasure-giving the son of Folcwalda
should honour the Danes day by day,
should distribute rings and gold-adorned gifts
to Hengest's band and his own people in equal measure.
Both sides pledged themselves to this peaceful
settlement. Finn swore Hengest solemn oaths

            * See Appendix VE.

that he would respect the sad survivors
as his counsellors ordained, and that no man there
must violate the covenant with word or deed,
or complain about it, although they
would be serving the slayer of their lord
(as fate had forced those lordless men to do);
and he warned the Frisians that if, in provocation,
they should mention the murderous feud,
the sword's edge should settle things.
The funeral fire was prepared, glorious gold
was brought up from the hoard: the best of Scyldings,
that race of warriors, lay ready on the pyre.
Blood-stained corslets, and images of boars
(cast in iron and covered in gold)
were plentiful on that pyre, and likewise the bodies
of many retainers, ravaged by wounds;
renowned men fell in that slaughter.
Then Hildeburh asked that her own son
be committed to the flames at her brother's funeral,
that his body be consumed on Hnæf's pyre.
That grief-stricken woman keened over his corpse,
sang doleful dirges. The warriors' voices
soared towards heaven. And so did the smoke
from the great funeral fire that roared
before the barrow; heads sizzled,
wounds split open, blood burst out
from battle scars. The ravenous flames
swallowed those men whole, made no distinction
between Frisians and Danes; the finest men departed.
Then those warriors, their friends lost to them,
went to view their homes, revisit the stronghold
and survey the Frisian land. But Hengest
stayed with Finn, in utter dejection, all through
that blood-stained winter. And he dreamed
of his own country, but he was unable to steer
his ship homeward, for the storm-beaten sea
wrestled with the wind; winter sheathed the waves

in ice — until once again spring made its sign
(as still it does) among the houses of men:
clear days, warm weather, in accordance as always
with the law of the seasons. Then winter was over,
the face of the earth was fair; the exile
was anxious to leave that foreign people
and the Frisian land. And yet he brooded
more about vengeance than about a voyage,
and wondered whether he could bring about a clash
so as to repay the sons of the Jutes.
Thus Hengest did not shrink from the duty of vengeance
after Hunlafing had placed the flashing sword,
finest of all weapons, on his lap;
this sword's edges had scarred many Jutes.
And so it was that cruel death by the sword later
cut down the brave warrior Finn in his own hall,
after Guthlaf and Oslaf, arrived from a sea-journey,
had fiercely complained of that first attack,
condemned the Frisians on many scores:
the Scyldings' restless spirits could no longer
be restrained. Then the hall ran red with the blood
of the enemy — Finn himself was slain,
the king with his troop, and Hildeburh was taken.
The Scylding warriors carried that king's
heirlooms down to their ship,
all the jewels and necklaces they discovered
at Finn's hall. They sailed over the sea-paths,
brought that noble lady back to Denmark
and her own people.
                    Thus was the lay sung,
the song of the poet. The hall echoed with joy,
waves of noise broke out along the benches;
cup-bearers carried wine in glorious vessels.
Then Wealhtheow, wearing her golden collar, walked
to where Hrothgar and Hrothulf were sitting side by side,
uncle and nephew, still friends together, true to one another.
And the spokesman Unferth sat at the feet

of the Danish lord; all men admired
his spirit and audacity, although he had deceived
his own kinsmen in a feud. Then the lady of the Scyldings
spoke these words: 'Accept this cup, my loved lord,
treasure-giver; O gold-friend of men,
learn the meaning of joy again, and speak words
of gratitude to the Geats, for so one ought to do.
And be generous to them too, mindful of gifts
which you have now amassed from far and wide.
I am told you intend to adopt this warrior,
take him for your son. This resplendent ring-hall,
Heorot, has been cleansed; give many rewards
while you may, but leave this land and the Danish people
to your own descendants when the day comes
for you to die. I am convinced
that gracious Hrothulf will guard our children
justly, should he outlive you, lord of the Scyldings,
in this world; I believe he will repay our sons
most generously if he remembers all we did
for his benefit and enjoyment when he was a boy.'
Then Wealhtheow walked to the bench where her sons,
Hrethric and Hrothmund, sat with the sons of thanes,
fledgling warriors; where also that brave man,
Beowulf of the Geats, sat beside the brothers.
To him she carried the cup, and asked in gracious words
if he would care to drink; and to him she presented
twisted gold with courtly ceremonial —
two armlets, a corslet and many rings,
and the most handsome collar in the world.
I have never heard that any hero had a jewel
to equal that, not since Hama made off
for his fortress with the Brosings' necklace, that pendant
in its precious setting; he fled from the enmity
of underhand Eormenric, he chose long-lasting gain.
Hygelac the Geat, grandson of Swerting,
wore that necklace on his last raid
when he fought beneath his banner to defend his treasure,

his battle spoils; fate claimed him then,
when he, foolhardy, courted disaster,
a feud with the Frisians. On that occasion the famous prince
had carried the treasure, the priceless stones,
over the cup of the waves; he crumpled under his shield.
Then the king's body fell into the hands of Franks,
his coat of mail and the collar also;
after that battle, weaker warriors picked at
and plundered the slain; many a Geat lay dead, guarding
that place of corpses.*

      Applause echoed in the hall.
Wealhtheow spoke these words before the company:
'May you, Beowulf, beloved youth, enjoy
with all good fortune this necklace and corslet,
treasures of the people; may you always prosper;
win renown through courage, and be kind in your counsel
to these boys; for that, I will reward you further.
You have ensured that men will always sing
your praises, even to the ends of the world,
as far as oceans still surround cliffs,
home of the winds. May you thrive, O prince,
all your life. I hope you will amass
a shining hoard of treasure. O happy Beowulf,
be gracious in your dealing with my sons.
Here, each warrior is true to the others,
gentle of mind, loyal to his lord;
the thanes are as one, the people all alert,
the warriors have drunk well. They will do as I ask.'
  Then Wealhtheow retired to her seat
beside her lord. That was the best of banquets,
men drank their fill of wine; they had not tasted
bitter destiny, the fate that had come and claimed
many of the heroes at the end of dark evenings,
when Hrothgar the warrior had withdrawn
to take his rest. Countless retainers
defended Heorot as they had often done before;

    * See Appendix VII.

benches were pushed back; the floor was padded
with beds and pillows. But one of the feasters
lying on his bed was doomed, and soon to die.
They set their bright battle-shields
at their heads. Placed on the bench
above each retainer, his crested helmet,
his linked corslet and sturdy spear-shaft
were plainly to be seen. It was their habit,
both at home and in the field,
to be prepared for battle always,
for any occasion their lord might need
assistance; that was a loyal band of retainers.

And so they slept. One man paid a heavy price
for his night's rest, as often happened
after Grendel first held the gold-hall
and worked his evil in it, until he met his doom,
death for his crimes. For afterwards it became clear,
and well known to the Scyldings, that some avenger
had survived the evil-doer, still lived after
that grievous, mortal combat.
                              Grendel's mother
was a monster of a woman; she mourned her fate —
she who had to live in the terrible lake,
the cold water streams, after Cain slew
his own brother, his father's son,
with a sword; he was outlawed after that;
a branded man, he abandoned human joys,
wandered in the wilderness. Many spirits, sent
by fate, issued from his seed; one of them, Grendel,
that hateful outcast, was surprised in the hall
by a vigilant warrior spoiling for a fight.
Grendel gripped and grabbed him there,
but the Geat remembered his vast strength,
that glorious gift given him of God,
and put his trust for support and assistance
in the grace of the Lord; thus he overcame
the envoy of hell, humbled his evil adversary.

So the joyless enemy of mankind journeyed
to the house of the dead. And then Grendel's mother,
mournful and ravenous, resolved to go
on a grievous journey to avenge her son's death.

Thus she reached Heorot; Ring-Danes, snoring,
were sprawled about the floor. The thanes suffered
a serious reverse as soon as Grendel's mother
entered the hall. The terror she caused,
compared to her son, equalled the terror
an Amazon inspires as opposed to a man,
when the ornamented sword, forged on the anvil,
the razor-sharp blade stained with blood,
shears through the boar-crested helmets of the enemy.
Then swords were snatched from benches, blades
drawn from scabbards, many a broad shield
was held firmly in the hall; none could don helmet
or spacious corslet — that horror caught them by surprise.
The monster wanted to make off for the moors,
fly for her life, as soon as she was found out.
Firmly she grasped one of the thanes
and made for the fens as fast as she could.
That man whom she murdered even as he slept
was a brave shield-warrior, a well-known thane,
most beloved by Hrothgar of all his hall retainers
between the two seas. Beowulf was not there;
the noble Geat had been allotted another lodging
after the giving of treasure earlier that evening.
Heorot was in uproar; she seized her son's
blood-crusted hand; anguish once again
had returned to the hall. What kind of bargain
was that, in which both sides forfeited
the lives of friends?
                    Then the old king,
the grizzled warrior, was convulsed with grief
when he heard of the death of his dearest retainer.

Immediately Beowulf, that man blessed with victory,
was called to the chamber of the king. At dawn

the noble warrior and his friends, his followers,
hurried to the room where the wise man was waiting,
waiting and wondering whether the Almighty
would ever allow an end to their adversity.
Then Beowulf, brave in battle, crossed
the floor with his band — the timbers thundered —
and greeted the wise king, overlord of Ing's
descendants; he asked if the night had passed off
peacefully, since his summons was so urgent.

    Hrothgar, guardian of the Scyldings, said:
'Do not speak of peace; grief once again
afflicts the Danish people. Yrmenlaf's
elder brother, Æschere, is dead,
my closest counsellor and my comrade,
my shoulder-companion when we shielded
our heads in the fight, when soldiers clashed on foot,
slashed at boar-crests. Æschere was all
that a noble man, a warrior should be.
The wandering, murderous monster slew him
in Heorot; and I do not know where that ghoul,
drooling at her feast of flesh and blood,
made off afterwards. She has avenged her son
whom you savaged yesterday with vice-like holds
because he had impoverished and killed my people
for many long years. He fell in mortal combat,
forfeit of his life; and now another mighty
evil ravager has come to avenge her kinsman;
and many a thane, mournful in his mind
for his treasure-giver, may feel she has avenged
that feud already, indeed more than amply;
now that hand lies still which once sustained you.

    I have heard my people say,
men of this country, counsellors in the hall,
that they have seen *two* such beings,
equally monstrous, rangers of the fell-country,
rulers of the moors; and these men assert
that so far as they can see one bears

a likeness to a woman; grotesque though he was,
the other who trod the paths of exile looked like a man,
though greater in height and build than a goliath;
he was christened *Grendel* by my people
many years ago; men do not know if he
had a father, a fiend once begotten
by mysterious spirits. These two live
in a little-known country, wolf-slopes, windswept headlands,
perilous paths across the boggy moors, where a mountain
    stream
plunges under the mist-covered cliffs,
rushes through a fissure. It is not far from here,
if measured in miles, that the lake stands
shadowed by trees stiff with hoar-frost.
A wood, firmly-rooted, frowns over the water.
There, night after night, a fearful wonder may be seen —
fire on the water; no man alive
is so wise as to know the nature of its depths.
Although the moor-stalker, the stag with strong horns,
when harried by hounds will make for the wood,
pursued from afar, he will succumb
to the hounds on the brink, rather than plunge in
and save his head. That is not a pleasant place.
When the wind arouses the wrath of the storm,
whipped waves rear up black from the lake,
reach for the skies, until the air becomes misty,
the heavens weep. Now, once again, help may be had
from you alone. As yet, you have not seen the haunt,
the perilous place where you may meet this most evil monster
face to face. Do you dare set eyes on it?
If you return unscathed, I will reward you
for your audacity, as I did before,
with ancient treasures and twisted gold.'
　　Beowulf, the son of Ecgtheow, answered:
'Do not grieve, wise Hrothgar! Better each man
should avenge his friend than deeply mourn.
The days on earth for every one of us

are numbered; he who may should win renown
before his death; that is a warrior's
best memorial when he has departed from this world.
Come, O guardian of the kingdom, let us lose
no time but track down Grendel's kinswoman.
I promise you that wherever she turns —
to honeycomb caves, to mountain woods,
to the bottom of the lake she shall find no refuge.
Shoulder your sorrows with patience
this day; this is what I expect of you.'

    Then the old king leaped up, poured out his gratitude
to God Almighty for the Geat's words.
Hrothgar's horse, his stallion with plaited mane,
was saddled and bridled; the wise ruler
set out in full array; his troop of shield-bearers
fell into step. They followed the tracks
along forest paths and over open hill-country
for mile after mile; the monster had made
for the dark moors directly, carrying the corpse
of the foremost thane of all those
who, with Hrothgar, had guarded the hall.
Then the man of noble lineage left Heorot far behind,
followed narrow tracks, string-thin paths
over steep, rocky slopes — remote parts
with beetling crags and many lakes
where water-demons lived. He went ahead
with a handful of scouts to explore the place;
all at once he came upon a dismal wood,
mountain trees standing on the edge
of a grey precipice; the lake lay beneath,
blood-stained and turbulent. The Danish retainers
were utterly appalled when they came upon
the severed head of their comrade Æschere
on the steep slope leading down to the lake;
all the thanes were deeply distressed.

    The water boiled with blood, with hot gore;
the warriors gaped at it. At times the horn sang

an eager battle-song. The brave men all sat down;
then they saw many serpents in the water,
strange sea-dragons swimming in the lake,
and also water-demons, lying on cliff-ledges,
monsters and serpents of the same kind
as often, in the morning, molest ships
on the sail-road. They plunged to the lake bottom,
bitter and resentful, rather than listen
to the song of the horn. The leader of the Geats
picked off one with his bow and arrow,
ended its life; the metal tip
stuck in its vitals; it swam more sluggishly
after that, as the life-blood ebbed from its body;
in no time this strange sea-dragon
bristled with barbed boar-spears, was subdued
and drawn up onto the cliff; men examined
that disgusting enemy.
                    Beowulf donned
his coat of mail, did not fear for his own life.
His massive corslet, linked by hand
and skilfully adorned, was to essay the lake —
it knew how to guard the body, the bone-chamber,
so that his foe's grasp, in its malicious fury,
could not crush his chest, squeeze out his life;
and his head was guarded by the gleaming helmet
which was to explore the churning waters,
stir their very depths; gold decorated it,
and it was hung with chain-mail, as the weapon smith
had wrought it long before, wondrously shaped it
and beset it with boar-images, so that
afterwards no battle-blade could do it damage.
Not least amongst his mighty aids was Hrunting,
the long-hilted sword Unferth lent him in his need;
it was one of the finest of heirlooms; the iron blade
was engraved with deadly, twig-like patterning,
tempered with battle blood. It had not failed
any of those men who had held it in their hands,

risked themselves on hazardous exploits,
pitted themselves against foes. That was not
the first time it had to do a hard day's work.
Truly, when Ecglaf's son, himself so strong,
lent that weapon to his better as a swordsman,
he had forgotten all those taunts he flung
when tipsy with wine; he dared not chance
his own arm under the breakers, dared not
risk his life; at the lake he lost
his renown for bravery. It was not so with Beowulf
once he had armed himself for battle.

The Geat, son of Ecgtheow, spoke:
'Great son of Healfdene, gracious ruler,
gold-friend of men, remember now —
for I am now ready to go —
what we agreed if I, fighting on your behalf,
should fail to return: that you would always
be like a father to me after I had gone.
Guard my followers, my dear friends,
if I die in battle; and, beloved Hrothgar,
send to Hygelac the treasures you gave me.
When the lord of the Geats, Hrethel's son,
sees those gifts of gold, he will know
that I found a noble giver of rings
and enjoyed his favour for as long as I lived.
And, O Hrothgar, let renowned Unferth
have the ancient treasure, the razor sharp
ornamented sword; and I will make my name
with Hrunting, or death will destroy me.'

After these words the leader of the Geats
dived bravely from the bank, did not even
wait for an answer; the seething water
received the warrior. A full day elapsed
before he could discern the bottom of the lake.

She who had guarded its length and breadth
for fifty years, vindictive, fiercely ravenous for blood,
soon realized that one of the race of men

was looking down into the monsters' lair.
Then she grasped him, clutched the Geat
in her ghastly claws; and yet she did not
so much as scratch his skin; his coat of mail
protected him; she could not penetrate
the linked metal rings with her loathsome fingers.
Then the sea-wolf dived to the bottom-most depths,
swept the prince to the place where she lived,
so that he, for all his courage, could not
wield a weapon; too many wondrous creatures
harassed him as he swam; many sea-serpents
with savage tusks tried to bore through his corslet,
the monsters molested him. Then the hero saw
that he had entered some loathsome hall
in which there was no water to impede him,
a vaulted chamber where the floodrush
could not touch him. A light caught his eye,
a lurid flame flickering brightly.
    Then the brave man saw the sea-monster,
fearsome, infernal; he whirled his blade,
swung his arm with all his strength,
and the ring-hilted sword sang a greedy war-song
on the monster's head. Then that guest realized
that his gleaming blade could not bite into her flesh,
break open her bone-chamber; its edge failed Beowulf
when he needed it; yet it had endured
many a combat, sheared often through the helmet,
split the corslet of a fated man; for the first time
that precious sword failed to live up to its name.
    Then, resolute, Hygelac's kinsman took his courage
in both hands, trusted in his own strength.
Angrily the warrior hurled Hrunting away,
the damascened sword with serpent patterns on its hilt;
tempered and steel-edged, it lay useless on the earth.
Beowulf trusted in his own strength,
the might of his hand. So must any man

who hopes to gain long-lasting fame
in battle; he must risk his life, regardless.
Then the prince of the Geats seized the shoulder
of Grendel's mother — he did not mourn their feud;
when they grappled, that brave man in his fury
flung his mortal foe to the ground.
Quickly she came back at him, locked him
in clinches and clutched at him fearsomely.
Then the greatest of warriors stumbled and fell.
She dropped on her hall-guest, drew her dagger,
broad and gleaming; she wanted to avenge her son,
her only offspring. The woven corslet
that covered his shoulders saved Beowulf's life,
denied access to both point and edge.
Then the leader of the Geats, Ecgtheow's son,
would have died far under the wide earth
had not his corslet, his mighty chain-mail,
guarded him, and had not holy God
granted him victory; the wise Lord,
Ruler of the Heavens, settled the issue
easily after the hero had scrambled to his feet.

   Then Beowulf saw among weapons an invincible sword
wrought by the giants, massive and double-edged,
the joy of many warriors; that sword was matchless,
well-tempered and adorned, forged in a finer age,
only it was so huge that no man but Beowulf
could hope to handle it in the quick of combat.
Ferocious in battle, the defender of the Scyldings
grasped the ringed hilt, swung the ornamented sword
despairing of his life — he struck such a savage blow
that the sharp blade slashed through her neck,
smashed the vertebrae; it severed her head
from the fated body; she fell at his feet.
The sword was bloodstained; Beowulf rejoiced.

   A light gleamed; the chamber was illumined
as if the sky's bright candle were shining
from heaven. Hygelac's thane inspected

the vaulted room, then walked round the walls,
fierce and resolute, holding the weapon firmly
by the hilt. The sword was not too large
for the hero's grasp, but he was eager to avenge
at once all Grendel's atrocities,
all the many visits the monster had inflicted
on the West-Danes — which began with the time
he slew Hrothgar's sleeping hearth-companions,
devoured fifteen of the Danish warriors
even as they slept, and carried off as many more,
a monstrous prize. But the resolute warrior
had already repaid him to such a degree
that he now saw Grendel lying on his death-bed,
his life's-blood drained because of the wound
he sustained in battle at Heorot. Then Grendel's corpse,
received a savage blow at the hero's hands,
his body burst open: Beowulf lopped off his head.

At once the wise men, anxiously gazing at
the lake with Hrothgar, saw that the water
had begun to chop and churn, that the waves
were stained with blood. The grey-haired Scyldings
discussed that bold man's fate, agreed
there was no hope of seeing that brave thane again —
no chance that he would come, rejoicing in victory,
before their renowned king; it seemed certain
to all but a few that the sea-wolf had destroyed him.

Then the ninth hour came. The noble Scyldings
left the headland; the gold-friend of men
returned to Heorot; the Geats, sick at heart,
sat down and stared at the lake.
Hopeless, they yet hoped to set eyes
on their dear lord.
                        Then the battle-sword
began to melt like a gory icicle
because of the monster's blood. Indeed,
it was a miracle to see it thaw entirely,
as does ice when the Father (He who ordains

all times and seasons) breaks the bonds of frost,
unwinds the flood fetters; He is the true Lord.
The leader of the Geats took none of the treasures
away from the chamber — though he saw many there —
except the monster's head and the gold-adorned
sword-hilt; the blade itself had melted,
the patterned sword had burnt, so hot was that blood,
so poisonous the monster who had died in the cave.
He who had survived the onslaught of his enemies
was soon on his way, swimming up through the water;
when the evil monster ended his days on earth,
left this transitory life, the troubled water
and all the lake's expanse was purged of its impurity.

Then the fearless leader of the seafarers
swam to the shore, exulting in his plunder,
the heavy burdens he had brought with him.
The intrepid band of thanes hurried towards him,
giving thanks to God, rejoicing
to see their lord safe and sound of limb.
The brave man was quickly relieved of his helmet
and corslet.
            The angry water under the clouds,
the lake stained with battle-blood, at last became calm.

Then they left the lake with songs on their lips,
retraced their steps along the winding paths
and narrow tracks; it was no easy matter
for those courageous men, bold as kings,
to carry the head away from the cliff
overlooking the lake. With utmost difficulty
four of the thanes bore Grendel's head
to the gold-hall on a battle-pole;
thus the fourteen Geats, unbroken
in spirit and eager in battle, very soon
drew near to Heorot; with them, that bravest
of brave men crossed the plain towards the mead-hall.
Then the fearless leader of the thanes,
covered with glory, matchless in battle,

once more entered Heorot to greet Hrothgar.
Grendel's head was carried by the hair
onto the floor where the warriors were drinking,
a ghastly thing paraded before the heroes and the queen.
Men stared at that wondrous spectacle.
  Beowulf, the son of Ecgtheow, said:
'So, son of Healfdene, lord of the Scyldings,
we proudly lay before you plunder from the lake;
this head you look at proves our success.
I barely escaped with my life from that combat
under the water, the risk was enormous;
our encounter would have ended at once if God
had not guarded me. Mighty though it is,
Hrunting was no use at all in the battle;
but the Ruler of men — how often He guides
the friendless one — granted that I
should see a huge ancestral sword hanging,
shining, on the wall; I unsheathed it.
Then, at the time destiny decreed, I slew
the warden of the hall. And when the blood,
the boiling battle-blood burst from her body,
that sword burnt, the damascened blade
was destroyed. I deprived my enemies
of that hilt; I repaid them as they deserved
for their outrages, murderous slaughter of the Danes.
I promise, then, O prince of the Scyldings,
that you can sleep in Heorot without anxiety,
rest with your retainers, with all the thanes
among your people — experienced warriors
and striplings together — without further fear
of death's shadow skulking near the hall.'
  Then the golden hilt, age-old work of giants,
was given to Hrothgar, the grizzled warrior,
the warlike lord; wrought by master-smiths,
it passed into the hands of the Danish prince
once the demons died; for that embittered fiend,
enemy of God, guilty of murder

had abandoned this world — and so had his mother.
Thus the hilt was possessed by the best
of earthly kings between the two seas,
the best of those who bestowed gold on Norse men.

Hrothgar spoke, first examining the hilt,
the ancient heirloom. On it was engraved
the origins of strife in time immemorial,
when the tide of rising water drowned
the race of giants; their end was horrible;
they were opposed to the Eternal Lord,
and their reward was the downpour and the flood.
Also, on the sword-guards of pure gold,
it was recorded in runic letters, as is the custom,
for whom that sword, finest of blades,
with twisted hilt and serpentine patterning
had first been made.   Then Healfdene's wise son
lifted his voice — everyone listened:
'This land's grizzled guardian, who promotes truth
and justice amongst his people, and forgets nothing
though the years pass, can say for certain that this man
is much favoured by fate! Beowulf my friend,
your name is echoed in every country
to earth's end. You wear your enormous might
with wisdom and with dignity. I shall keep
my promise made when last we spoke. You will
beyond doubt be the shield of the Geats
for days without number, and a source
of strength to warriors.   Heremod* was hardly that
to Ecgwala's sons, the glorious Scyldings;
he grew to spread slaughter and destruction
rather than happiness amongst the Danish people.
In mad rage he murdered his table-companions,
his most loyal followers; it came about
that the great prince cut himself off

                    * See Appendix VD.

from all earthly pleasures, though God had endowed him
with strength and power above all other men,
and had sustained him. For all that, his heart
was filled with savage blood-lust. He never gave
gifts to the Danes, to gain glory. He lived joyless,
agony racked him; he was long an affliction
to his people. Be warned, Beowulf,
learn the nature of nobility. I who tell you
this story am many winters old.
                              It is a miracle
how the mighty Lord in his generosity
gives wisdom and land and high estate
to people on earth; all things are in His power.
At times he allows a noble man's mind to experience
happiness, grants he should rule over a pleasant,
prosperous country, a stronghold of men,
makes subject to him regions of earth,
a wide kingdom, until in his stupidity
there is no end to his ambition.
His life is unruffled — neither old age
nor illness afflict him, no unhappiness
gnaws at his heart, in his land no hatred
flares up in mortal feuds, but all the world
bends to his will. He suffers no setbacks
until the seed of arrogance is sown and grows
within him, while still the watchman slumbers;
how deeply the soul's guardian sleeps
when a man is enmeshed in matters of this world;
the evil archer stands close with his drawn bow,
his bristling quiver. Then the poisoned shaft
pierces his mind under his helmet
and he does not know how to resist
the devil's insidious, secret temptations.
What had long contented him now seems insufficient;
he becomes embittered, begins to hoard
his treasures, never parts with gold rings
in ceremonial splendour; he soon forgets

his destiny and disregards the honours
given him of God, the Ruler of Glory.
In time his transient body wizens and withers,
and dies as fate decrees; then another man
succeeds to his throne who gives treasures and heirlooms
with great generosity; *he* is not obsessed with suspicions.
Arm yourself, dear Beowulf, best of men,
against such diseased thinking; always swallow pride;
remember, renowned warrior, what is more worthwhile —
gain everlasting. Today and tomorrow
you will be in your prime; but soon you will die,
in battle or in bed; either fire or water,
the fearsome elements, will embrace you,
or you will succumb to the sword's flashing edge,
or the arrow's flight, or terrible old age;
then your eyes, once bright, will be clouded over;
all too soon, O warrior, death will destroy you.
      I have ruled the Ring-Danes under the skies
for fifty years, shielded them in war
from many tribes of men in this world,
from swords and from ash-spears, and the time had come
when I thought I had no enemies left on earth.
All was changed utterly, gladness
became grief, after Grendel,
my deadly adversary, invaded Heorot.
His visitations caused me continual pain.
Thus I thank the Creator, the Eternal Lord,
that after our afflictions I have lived to see,
to see with my own eyes this blood-stained head.
Now, Beowulf, brave in battle,
go to your seat and enjoy the feast;
tomorrow we shall share many treasures.'
      The Geat, full of joy, straightway went
to find his seat as Hrothgar had suggested.
Then, once again, as so often before,
a great feast was prepared for the brave warriors

sitting in the hall.
                                The shadows of night
settled over the retainers. The company arose;
the grey-haired man, the old Scylding,
wanted to retire. And the Geat, the shield-warrior,
was utterly exhausted, his bones ached for sleep.
At once the chamberlain — he who courteously
saw to all such needs as a thane,
a travelling warrior, had in those days —
showed him, so limb-weary, to his lodging.

Then Beowulf rested; the building soared,
spacious and adorned with gold; the guest
slept within until the black raven gaily
proclaimed sunrise. Bright light
chased away the shadows of night.
                                Then the warriors
hastened, the thanes were eager to return
to their own people; the brave seafarer
longed to see his ship, so far from that place.
Then the bold Geat ordered that Hrunting,
that sword beyond price, be brought before Unferth;
he begged him to take it back and thanked him
for the loan of it; he spoke of it as an ally
in battle, and assured Unferth he did not
underrate it: what a brave man he was!
After this the warriors, wearing their chain-mail,
were eager to be off; their leader,
so dear to the Danes, walked to the daïs
where Hrothgar was sitting, and greeted him.

Beowulf, the son of Ecgtheow, spoke:
'Now we seafarers, who have sailed here from far,
beg to tell you we are eager
to return to Hygelac. We have been happy here,
hospitably entertained; you have treated us kindly.
If I can in any way win more of your affection,
O ruler of men, than I have done already,
I will come at once, eager for combat.
If news reaches me over the seas

that you are threatened by those around you
(just as before enemies endangered you)
I will bring thousands of thanes,
all heroes, to help you. I know that Hygelac,
lord of the Geats, guardian of his people,
will advance me in word and deed
although he is young, so that I can back
these promises with spear shafts, and serve you
with all my strength where you need men.
Should Hrethric, Hrothgar's son, wish
to visit the court of the Geatish king,
he will be warmly welcomed. Strong men
should seek fame in far-off lands.'

   Hrothgar replied: 'The wise Lord put these words
into your mind; I have never heard a warrior
speak more sagely while still so young.
You are very strong and very shrewd,
you speak with discerning. If your leader,
Hrethel's son, guardian of the people,
were to lose his life by illness or by iron,
by spear or grim swordplay, and if you survived him,
it seems to me that the Geats could not choose
a better man for king, should you wish to rule
the land of your kinsmen. Beloved Beowulf,
the longer I know you, the greater my regard for you.
Because of your exploit, your act of friendship,
there will be an end to the gross outrages,
the old enmity between Geats and Danes;
they will learn to live in peace.
For as long as I rule this spacious land,
heirlooms will be exchanged; many men
will greet their friends with gifts, send them
over the seas where gannets swoop and rise;
the ring-prowed ship will take tokens of esteem,
treasures across the waters. I know the Geats
are honourable to friend and foe alike,
always faithful to their ancient code.'

Then Healfdene's son, guardian of thanes,
gave him twelve treasures in the hall,
told him to go safely with those gifts
to his own dear kinsmen, and to come back soon.
That king, descendant of kings,
leader of the Scyldings, kissed and embraced
the best of thanes; tears streamed down
the old man's face. The more that warrior thought,
wise and old, the more it seemed
improbable that they would meet again,
brave men in council. He so loved Beowulf
that he could not conceal his sense of loss;
but in his heart and in his head,
in his very blood, a deep love burned
for that dear man.
              Then Beowulf the warrior,
proudly adorned with gold, crossed the plain,
exulting in his treasure. The ship
rode at anchor, waiting for its owner.
Then, as they walked, they often praised
Hrothgar's generosity. He was an altogether
faultless king, until old age deprived him
of his strength, as it does most men.

Then that troop of brave young retainers
came to the water's edge; they wore ring-mail,
woven corslets. And the same watchman
who had seen them arrive saw them now returning.
He did not insult them, ask for explanations,
but galloped from the cliff-top to greet the guests;
he said that those warriors in gleaming armour,
so eager to embark, would be welcomed home.
Then the spacious ship, with its curved prow,
standing ready on the shore, was laden with armour,
with horses and treasure. The mast towered
over Hrothgar's precious heirlooms.

Beowulf gave a sword bound round with gold
to the ship's watchman — a man who thereafter

was honoured on the mead-bench that much the more
on account of this heirloom.

                    The ship surged forward,
butted the waves in deep waters;
it drew away from the shores of the Scyldings.
Then a sail, a great sea-garment, was fastened
with guys to the mast; the timbers groaned;
the boat was not blown off its course
by the stiff sea-breezes. The ship swept
over the waves; foaming at the bows,
the boat with its well-wrought prow sped
over the waters, until at last the Geats
set eyes on the cliffs of their own country,
the familiar headlands; the vessel pressed forward,
pursued by the wind — it ran up onto dry land.

    The harbour guardian hurried down to the shore;
for many days he had scanned the horizon,
anxious to see those dear warriors once more.
He tethered the spacious sea-steed with ropes
(it rode on its painter restlessly)
so that the rolling waves could not wrench it away.
Then Beowulf commanded that the peerless treasures,
the jewels and plated gold, be carried up from the shore.
He had not to go far to find the treasure-giver,
Hygelac son of Hrethel, for his house and the hall
for his companions stood quite close to the sea-wall.
That high hall was a handsome building;
it became the valiant king.

                    Hygd, his queen,
Hæreth's daughter, was very young; but she
was discerning, and versed in courtly customs,
though she had lived a short time only
in that citadel; and she was not too thrifty,
not ungenerous with gifts of precious treasures
to the Geatish thanes.

                Queen Thryth* was proud

        * See Appendix VF.

and perverse, pernicious to her people.
No hero but her husband, however bold,
dared by day so much as turn his head
in her direction — that was far too dangerous;
but, if he did, he could bargain on being cruelly
bound with hand-plaited ropes; soon
after his seizure, the blade was brought into play,
the damascened sword to settle the issue,
to inflict death. It is not right for a queen,
compelling though her beauty, to behave like this,
for a peace-weaver to deprive a dear man of his life
because she fancies she has been insulted.
But Offa, Hemming's kinsman, put an end to that.
Ale-drinking men in the hall have said
that she was no longer perfidious to her people,
and committed no crimes, once she had been given,
adorned with gold, to that young warrior
of noble descent — once she had sailed,
at her father's command, to Offa's court
beyond the pale gold sea. After that,
reformed, she turned her life to good account;
renowned for virtue, she reigned with vision;
and she loved the lord of warriors in the high way
of love — he who was, as I have heard,
the best of all men, the mighty human race,
between the two seas. Offa the brave
was widely esteemed both for his gifts
and his skill in battle; he ruled his land
wisely. He fathered Eomer, guardian
of thanes, who was Hemming's kinsman,
grandson of Garmund, a goliath in battle.

Then Beowulf and his warrior band walked
across the sand, tramped over
the wide foreshore; the world's candle shone,
the sun hastening from the south. The men hurried too
when they were told that the guardian of thanes,
Ongentheow's slayer, the excellent young king,

held court in the hall, distributing rings.
Hygelac was informed at once of Beowulf's arrival —
that the shield of warriors, his comrade in battle,
had come back alive to the fortified enclosure,
was heading for the hall unscathed after combat.
Space on the benches for Beowulf and his band
was hastily arranged, as Hygelac ordered.
    The guardian of thanes formally greeted
that loyal man; then they sat down —
the unfated hero opposite the king,
kinsman facing kinsman. Hæreth's daughter
carried mead-cups round the hall,
spoke kindly to the warriors, handed the stoups
of wine to the thanes. Hygelac began
to ask his companion courteous questions
in the high hall; he was anxious to hear
all that had happened to the seafaring Geats:
'Beloved Beowulf, tell me what became of you
after the day you so hurriedly decided
to do battle far from here over the salt waters,
to fight at Heorot. And were you able
to assuage the grief, the well-known sorrow
of glorious Hrothgar? Your undertaking
deeply troubled me; I despaired, dear Beowulf,
of your return. I pleaded with you
not on any account to provoke that monster,
but to let the South-Danes settle their feud
with Grendel themselves. God be praised
that I am permitted to see you safe and home.'
    Then Beowulf, the son of Ecgtheow, said:
'Half the world, lord Hygelac, has heard
of my encounter, my great combat
hand to hand with Grendel in that hall
where he had harrowed and long humiliated
the glorious Scyldings. I avenged it all;
none of Grendel's brood, however long
the last of that hateful race survives,

steeped in crime, has any cause to boast about
that dawn combat.
                              First of all,
I went to the ring-hall to greet Hrothgar;
once Healfdene's great son knew of my intentions,
he assigned me a seat beside his own sons.
Then there was revelry; never in my life,
under heaven's vault, have I seen men
happier in the mead-hall. From time to time
the famous queen, the peace-weaver, walked across the
     floor,
exhorting the young warriors; often she gave
some man a twisted ring before returning to her seat.
At times Hrothgar's daughter, whom I heard
men call Freawaru, carried the ale-horn
right round the hall in front of that brave company,
offered that vessel adorned with precious metals
to the thirsty warriors.
                              Young, and decorated
with gold ornaments, she is promised to Froda's noble son,
Ingeld of the Heathobards; that match was arranged
by the lord of the Scyldings, guardian of the kingdom;
he believes that it is an excellent plan
to use her as a peace-weaver to bury old antagonisms,
mortal feuds. But the deadly spear rarely sleeps
for long after a prince lies dead in the dust,
however exceptional the bride may be!
   For Ingeld, leader of the Heathobards, and all
his retainers will later be displeased when he
and Freawaru walk on the floor — man and wife —
and when Danish warriors are being entertained.
For the guests will gleam with Heathobard heirlooms,
iron-hard, adorned with rings,
precious possessions that had belonged
to their hosts' fathers for as long as they
could wield their weapons, until in the shield-play
they and their dear friends forfeited their lives.

Then, while men are drinking, an old
warrior will speak; a sword he has seen,
marvellously adorned, stirs his memory
of how Heathobards were slain by spears;
he seethes with fury; sad in his heart,
he begins to taunt a young Heathobard,
incites him to action with these words:
   "Do you not recognize that sword, my friend,
the sword your father, fully armed, bore into battle
that last time, when he was slain by Danes,
killed by brave Scyldings who carried the field
when Withergyld fell and many warriors beside him?
See how the son of one of those
who slew him struts about the hall;
he sports the sword; he crows about that slaughter,
and carries that heirloom which is yours by right!"
In this way, with acid words, he will endlessly
provoke him and rake up the past,
until the time will come when a Danish warrior,
Freawaru's thane, sleeps blood-stained,
slashed by the sword, punished by death
for the deeds of his father; and the Heathobard
will escape, well-acquainted with the country.
Then both sides will break the solemn oath
sworn by their leaders; and Ingeld will come
to hate the Scyldings, and his love for his wife
will no longer be the same after such anguish and grief.
Thus I have little faith in friendship with Heathobards;
they will fail to keep their side of the promise,
friendship with the Danes.
                      I have digressed;
Grendel is my subject. Now you must hear,
O treasure-giver, what the outcome was
of that hand-to-hand encounter. When the jewel of heaven
had journeyed over the earth, the angry one,
the terrible night-prowler paid us a visit —
unscathed warriors watching over Heorot.

A fight awaited Hondscio, a horrible end
for that fated man; he was the first to fall;
Grendel tore that famous young retainer to bits
between his teeth, and swallowed the whole body
of that dear man, that girded warrior.
And even then that murderer, mindful of evil,
his mouth caked with blood, was not content
to leave the gold-hall empty-handed
but, famed for his strength, he tackled me,
gripped me with his outstretched hand.
A huge unearthly glove swung at his side,
firmly secured with subtle straps;
it had been made with great ingenuity,
with devils' craft and dragons' skins.
Innocent as I was, the demon monster
meant to shove me in it, and many another
innocent besides; that was beyond him
after I leapt up, filled with fury.
It would take too long to tell you how I repaid
that enemy of men for all his outrages;
but there, my prince, I ennobled your people
with my deeds. Grendel escaped,
and lived a little longer; but he left
behind at Heorot his right hand; and, in utter
wretchedness, sank to the bottom of the lake.

  The sun rose; we sat down together
to feast, then the leader of the Scyldings
paid a good price for the bloody battle,
gave me many a gold-plated treasure.
There was talk and song; the grey-haired Scylding
opened his immense hoard of memories;
now and then a happy warrior touched
the wooden harp, reciting some story,
mournful and true; at times the generous king
recalled in proper detail some strange incident;
and as the shadows lengthened, an aged thane,
cramped and rheumatic, raised his voice

time and again, lamenting his lost youth,
his prowess in battle; worn with winters,
his heart quickened to the call of the past.

In these ways we relaxed agreeably
throughout the long day until darkness closed in,
another night for men. Then, in her grief,
bent on vengeance, Grendel's mother
hastened to the hall where death had lain
in wait for her son — the battle-hatred
of the Geats. The horrible harridan avenged
her offspring, slew a warrior brazenly.
Æschere, the wise old counsellor, lost
his life. And when morning came,
the Danes were unable to cremate him,
to place the body of that dear man
on the funeral pyre; for Grendel's mother
had carried it off in her gruesome grasp,
taken it under the mountain lake.
Of all the grievous sorrows Hrothgar
long sustained, none was more terrible.
Then the king in his anger called upon your name
and entreated me to risk my life,
to accomplish deeds of utmost daring
in the tumult of waves; he promised me rewards.
And so, as men now know all over the earth,
I found the grim guardian of the lake-bottom.
For a while we grappled; the water boiled
with blood; then in that battle-hall,
I lopped off Grendel's mother's head
with the mighty sword. I barely escaped
with my life; but I was not fated.

And afterwards the guardian of thanes,
Healfdene's son, gave me many treasures.
Thus the king observed excellent tradition:
in no wise did I feel unrewarded
for all my efforts, but Healfdene's son
offered me gifts of my own choosing;

gifts, O noble king, I wish now
to give to you in friendship. I still depend
entirely on your favours; I have few
close kinsmen but you, O Hygelac!'
     Then Beowulf caused to be brought in
a standard bearing the image of a boar,
together with a helmet towering in battle,
a grey corslet, and a noble sword; he said:
'Hrothgar, the wise king, gave me
these trappings and purposely asked me
to tell you their history: he said that Heorogar,
lord of the Scyldings, long owned them.
Yet he has not endowed his own brave son,
Heoroweard, with this armour, much as
he loves him. Make good use of everything!'
     I heard that four bays, apple-brown,
were brought into the hall after the armour —
swift as the wind, identical. Beowulf gave them
as he gave the treasures. So should a kinsman do,
and never weave nets with underhand subtlety
to ensnare others, never have designs
on a close comrade's life. His nephew,
brave in battle, was loyal to Hygelac;
each man was mindful of the other's pleasure.
     I heard that he gave Hygd the collar,
the wondrous ornament with which Wealhtheow,
daughter of the prince, had presented him,
and gave her three horses also, graceful creatures
with brightly-coloured saddles; Hygd
wore that collar, her breast was adorned.
     Thus Ecgtheow's son, feared in combat,
confirmed his courage with noble deeds;
he lived a life of honour, he never slew
companions at the feast; savagery was
alien to him, but he, so brave in battle,
made the best use of those ample talents
with which God endowed him.

He had been despised
for a long while, for the Geats saw no spark
of bravery in him, nor did their king deem him
worthy of much attention on the mead-bench;
people thought that he was a sluggard,
a feeble princeling. How fate changed,
changed completely for that glorious man!

Then the guardian of thanes, the famous king,
ordered that Hrethel's gold-adorned heirloom
be brought in; no sword was so treasured
in all Geatland; he laid it in Beowulf's lap,
and gave him seven thousand hides of land,
a hall and princely throne. Both men
had inherited land and possessions
in that country; but the more spacious kingdom
had fallen to Hygelac, who was of higher rank.

In later days, after much turmoil,
things happened in this way: when Hygelac lay dead
and murderous battle-blades had beaten down
the shield of his son Heardred,
and when the warlike Swedes, savage warriors,
had hunted him down amongst his glorious people,
attacked Hereric's nephew with hatred,
the great kingdom of the Geats passed
into Beowulf's hands.* He had ruled it well
for fifty winters — he was a wise king,
a grizzled guardian of the land — when, on dark nights,
a dragon began to terrify the Geats:
he lived on a cliff, kept watch over a hoard
in a high stone barrow; below, there was
a secret path; a man strayed
into this barrow by chance, seized
some of the pagan treasures, stole drinking vessels.
At first the sleeping dragon was deceived

* On the Geatish–Swedish Wars, see Appendix VII.

by the thief's skill, but afterwards he avenged
this theft of gleaming gold; people far and wide,
bands of retainers, became aware of his wrath.
    That man did not intrude upon the hoard
deliberately, he who robbed the dragon;
but it was some slave, a wanderer in distress
escaping from men's anger who entered there,
seeking refuge. He stood guilty of some sin.
As soon as he peered in, the outsider
stiffened with horror. Unhappy as he was,
he stole the vessel, the precious cup.
There were countless heirlooms in that earth-cave,
the enormous legacy of a noble people,
ancient treasures which some man or other
had cautiously concealed there many years
before. Death laid claim to all that people
in days long past, and then that retainer
who outlived the rest, a gold-guardian
mourning his friends, expected the same fate —
thought he would enjoy those assembled heirlooms
a little while only. A newly-built barrow
stood ready on a headland which overlooked
the sea, protected by the hazards of access.
To this barrow the protector of rings brought the heirlooms,
the plated gold, all that part of the precious treasure
worthy of hoarding; then he spoke a few words:
'Hold now, O earth, since heroes could not,
these treasures owned by nobles! Indeed, strong men
first quarried them from you. Death in battle,
ghastly carnage, has claimed all my people —
men who once made merry in the hall
have laid down their lives; I have no one
to carry the sword, to polish the plated vessel,
this precious drinking-cup; all the retainers
have hurried elsewhere. The iron helmet
adorned with gold shall lose its ornaments;

men who should polish battle-masks are sleeping;
the coat of mail, too, that once withstood
the bite of swords in battle, after shields were shattered,
decays like the warriors; the linked mail may no longer
range far and wide with the warrior,
stand side by side with heroes. Gone is the pleasure
of plucking the harp, no fierce hawk
swoops about the hall, nor does the swift stallion
strike sparks in the courtyard. Cruel death
has claimed hundreds of this human race.'*

    Thus the last survivor mourned time passing,
and roamed about by day and night,
sad and aimless, until death's lightning
struck at his heart.

                The aged dragon of darkness
discovered that glorious hoard unguarded,
he who sought out barrows, smooth-scaled
and evil, and flew by night, breathing
fire; the Geats feared him greatly.
He was destined to find the hoard
in that cave and, old in winters, guard
the heathen gold; much good it did him!

    Thus the huge serpent who harassed men
guarded that great stronghold under the earth
for three hundred winters, until
a man enraged him; the wanderer carried
the inlaid vessel to his lord, and begged him
for a bond of peace. Then the hoard was raided
and plundered, and that unhappy man
was granted his prayer. His lord examined
the ancient work of smiths for the first time.

    There was conflict once more after the dragon
awoke; intrepid, he slid swiftly
along by the rock, and found the footprints
of the intruder; that man had skilfully
picked his way right past the dragon's head.

    * The original of this passage is printed and discussed in Appendix IIc.

Thus he who is undoomed will easily survive
anguish and exile provided he enjoys
the grace of God. The warden of the hoard
prowled up and down, anxious to find
the man who had pillaged it while he slept.
Breathing fire and filled with fury,
he circled the outside of the earth mound
again and again; but there was no one
in that barren place; yet he exulted at the thought
of battle, bloody conflict; at times he wheeled back
into the barrow, hunting for the priceless heirloom.
He realized at once that one of the race of men
had discovered the gold, the glorious treasure.
Restlessly the dragon waited for darkness;
the guardian of the hoard was bursting with rage,
he meant to avenge the vessel's theft
with fire.
      Then daylight failed
as the dragon desired; he could no longer
confine himself to the cave but flew in a ball
of flame, burning for vengeance. The Geats
were filled with dread as he began his flight;
it swiftly ended in disaster for their lord.
    Then the dragon began to breathe forth fire,
to burn fine buildings; flame tongues flickered,
terrifying men; the loathsome winged creature
meant to leave the whole place lifeless.
Everywhere the violence of the dragon, the venom
of that hostile one, was clearly to be seen —
how he had wrought havoc, hated and humiliated
the Geatish people. Then, before dawn he rushed back
to his hidden lair and the treasure hoard.
He had girdled the Geats with fire,
with ravening flames; he relied on his own strength,
and on the barrow and the cliff; his trust played him false.
    Then news of that terror was quickly brought
to Beowulf, that flames enveloped

his own hall, best of buildings,
and the gift-throne of the Geats. That good man
was choked with intolerable grief.
Wise that he was, he imagined
he must have angered God, the Lord Eternal,
by ignoring some ancient law; he was seldom
dispirited, but now his heart was like lead.

The fire dragon had destroyed the fortified hall,
the people's stronghold, and laid waste with flames
the land by the sea. The warlike king,
prince of the Geats, planned to avenge this.
The protector of warriors, leader of men,
instructed the smith to forge a curious shield
made entirely of iron; he well knew
that a linden shield would not last long
against the flames. The eminent prince
was doomed to reach the end of his days on earth,
his life in this world. So too was the dragon,
though he had guarded the hoard for generations.

Then the giver of gold disdained
to track the dragon with a troop
of warlike men; he did not shrink
from single combat, nor did he set much store
by the fearless dragon's power, for had he not before
experienced danger, again and again
survived the storm of battle, beginning with that time
when, blessed with success, he cleansed
Hrothgar's hall, and crushed in battle
the monster and his vile mother?

                              That grim combat
in which Hygelac was slain — Hrethel's son,
leader of the Geats, dear lord of his people,
struck down by swords in the bloodbath
in Frisia — was far from the least
of his encounters. Beowulf escaped
because of his skill and stamina at swimming;
he waded into the water, bearing no fewer

than thirty corslets, a deadweight on his arms.
But the Frankish warriors who shouldered
their shields against him had no cause to boast
about that combat; a handful only
eluded that hero and returned home.
Then the son of Ecgtheow, saddened and alone,
rode with the white horses to his own people.
Hygd offered him heirlooms there, and even
the kingdom, the ancestral throne itself; for she feared
that her son would be unable to defend it
from foreign invaders now that Hygelac was gone.
But the Geats, for all their anguish, failed
to prevail upon the prince — he declined
absolutely to become Heardred's lord,
or to taste the pleasures of royal power.
But he stood at his right hand,
ready with advice, always friendly,
and respectful, until the boy came of age
and could rule the Geats himself.

                            Two exiles,
Ohthere's sons, sailed to Heardred's court;
they had rebelled against the ruler of the Swedes,
a renowned man, the best of sea-kings,
gold-givers in Sweden. By receiving them,
Heardred rationed the days of his life;
in return for his hospitality, Hygelac's son
was mortally wounded, slashed by swords.
Once Heardred lay lifeless in the dust,
Onela, son of Ongentheow, sailed home again;
he allowed Beowulf to inherit the throne
and rule the Geats; he was a noble king!
But Beowulf did not fail with help
after the death of the prince, although years passed;
he befriended unhappy Eadgils, Ohthere's son,
and supplied him with weapons and warriors
beyond the wide seas. Eadgils afterwards
avenged Eanmund, he ravaged and savaged

the Swedes, and killed the king, Onela himself.
    Thus the son of Ecgtheow had survived
these feuds, these fearful battles, these acts
of single combat, up to that day
when he was destined to fight against the dragon.
Then in fury the leader of the Geats set out
with eleven to search for the winged serpent.
By then Beowulf knew the cause of the feud,
bane of men; the famous cup
had come to him through the hands of its finder.
The unfortunate slave who first brought about
such strife made the thirteenth man
in that company — cowed and disconsolate,
he had to be their guide. Much against his will,
he conducted them to the entrance of the cave,
an earth-hall full of filigree work
and fine adornments close by the sea,
the fretting waters. The vile guardian,
the serpent who had long lived under the earth,
watched over the gold, alert; he who hoped
to gain it bargained with his own life.
    Then the brave king sat on the headland,
the gold-friend of the Geats wished success
to his retainers. His mind was most mournful,
angry, eager for slaughter; fate hovered
over him, so soon to fall on that old man,
to seek out his hidden spirit, to split
life and body; flesh was to confine
the soul of the king only a little longer.
Beowulf, the son of Ecgtheow, spoke:
'Often and often in my youth I plunged
into the battle maelstrom; how well I remember it.
I was seven winters old when the treasure guardian,
ruler of men, received me from my father.
King Hrethel took me into his ward, reared me,
fed me, gave me gold, mindful of our kinship;
for as long as he lived, he loved me no less

than his own three sons, warriors with me
in the citadel, Herebeald, Hæthcyn, and my dear Hygelac.
A death-bed for the firstborn was unrolled
most undeservedly by the action of his kinsman —
Hæthcyn drew his horn-tipped bow
and killed his lord-to-be; he missed his mark,
his arrow was stained with his brother's blood.
That deed was a dark sin, sickening
to think of, not to be settled by payment of *wergild*;
yet Herebeald's death could not be requited.
   Thus the old king, Hrethel, is agonized
to see his son, so young, swing
from the gallows.* He sings a dirge, a song
dark with sorrow, while his son hangs,
raven's carrion, and he cannot help him
in any way, wise and old as he is.
He wakes each dawn to the ache
of his son's death; he has no desire
for a second son, to be his heir
in the stronghold, now that his firstborn
has finished his days and deeds on earth.
Grieving, he wanders through his son's dwelling,
sees the wine-hall now deserted, joyless,
home of the winds; the riders, the warriors,
sleep in their graves. No longer is the harp
plucked, no longer is there happiness in that place.
Then Hrethel takes to his bed, and intones
dirges for his dead son, Herebeald;
his house and his lands seem empty now,
and far too large. Thus the lord of the Geats
endured in his heart the ebb and flow
of sorrow for his firstborn; but he could not
avenge that feud on the slayer — his own son;
although Hrethel had no love for Hæthcyn,
he could no more readily requite death

---

* This is perhaps best explained as a reference to a ritual, sacrificial hanging on the gallows of one who did not die in battle.

with death. Such was his sorrow that he lost
all joy in life, chose the light of God;
he bequeathed to his sons, as a wealthy man does,
his citadel and land, when he left this life.
    Then there was strife, savage conflict
between Swedes and Geats; after Hrethel's death
the feud we shared, the fierce hatred
flared up across the wide water.
The sons of Ongentheow, Onela and Ohthere,
were brave and battle-hungry; they had no wish
for peace over the sea but several times,
and wantonly, butchered the people of the Geats
on the slopes of Slaughter Hill.* As is well known,
my kinsmen requited that hatred, those crimes;
but one of them paid with his own life —
a bitter bargain; that fight was fatal
to Hæthcyn, ruler of the Geats.
Then I heard that in the morning
one kinsman avenged another, repaid
Hæthcyn's slayer with the battle-blade,
when Ongentheow attacked the Geat Eofor;
the helmet split, the old Swede fell,
pale in death; Eofor remembered
that feud well enough, his hand and sword
spared nothing in their death-swing.
    I repaid Hygelac for his gifts of heirlooms
with my gleaming blade, repaid him in battle,
as was granted to me; he gave me land
and property, a happy home. He had
no need to hunt out and hire mercenaries —
inferior warriors from the Gepidae,
from the Spear-Danes or from tribes in Sweden;
but I was always at the head of his host,
alone in the van; and I shall still fight
for as long as I live and this sword lasts,
that has often served me early and late

    * A poetic licence for the Old English *Hrēosnabeorh*.

since I became the daring slayer
of Dæghrefn, champion of the Franks.
He was unable to bring adornments,
breast-decorations to the Frisian king,
but fell in the fight bearing the standard,
a brave warrior; it was my battle-grip,
not the sharp blade, that shattered his bones,
silenced his heartbeat. Now the shining edge,
hand and tempered sword, shall engage in battle
for the treasure hoard. I fought many battles
when I was young; yet I will fight again,
the old guardian of my people, and achieve
a mighty exploit if the evil dragon dares
confront me, dares come out of the earth-cave!'

    Then he addressed each of the warriors,
the brave heroes, his dear companions,
a last time: 'I would not wield a sword
against the dragon if I could grasp this hideous being
with my hands (and thus make good my boast),
as once I grasped the monster Grendel;
but I anticipate blistering battle-fire,
venomous breath; therefore I have with me
my shield and corslet. I will not give an inch
to the guardian of the mound, but at that barrow
it will befall us both as fate ordains,
every man's master. My spirit is bold,
I will not boast further against the fierce flier.
Watch from the barrow, warriors in armour,
guarded by corslets, which of us will better
weather his wounds after the combat.
This is not your undertaking, nor is it
possible for any man but me alone
to pit his strength against the gruesome one,
and perform great deeds. I will gain the gold
by daring, or else battle, dread destroyer
of life, will lay claim to your lord.'

    Then the bold warrior, stern-faced beneath his helmet,

stood up with his shield; sure of his own strength,
he walked in his corslet towards the cliff;
the way of the coward is not thus!
Then that man endowed with noble qualities,
he who had braved countless battles, weathered
the thunder when warrior troops clashed together,
saw a stone arch set in the cliff
through which a stream spurted; steam rose
from the boiling water; he could not stay long
in the hollow near the hoard for fear
of being scorched by the dragon's flames.
Then, such was his fury, the leader of the Geats
threw out his chest and gave a great roar,
the brave man bellowed; his voice, renowned
in battle, hammered the grey rock's anvil.
The guardian of the hoard knew the voice for human;
violent hatred stirred within him. Now no time
remained to entreat for peace. At once
the monster's breath, burning battle vapour,
issued from the barrow; the earth itself snarled.
The lord of the Geats, standing under the cliff,
raised his shield against the fearsome stranger;
then that sinuous creature spoiled
for the fight. The brave and warlike king
had already drawn his keen-edged sword,
(it was an ancient heirloom); a terror of each other
lurked in the hearts of the two antagonists.
While the winged creature coiled himself up,
the friend and lord of men stood unflinching
by his shield; Beowulf waited ready armed.
    Then, fiery and twisted, the dragon swiftly
shrithed towards its fate. The shield protected
the life and body of the famous prince
for far less time than he had looked for.
It was the first occasion in all his life
that fate did not decree triumph for him
in battle. The lord of the Geats raised

his arm, and struck the mottled monster
with his vast ancestral sword; but the bright blade's
edge was blunted by the bone, bit
less keenly than the desperate king required.
The defender of the barrow bristled with anger
at the blow, spouted murderous fire, so that flames
leaped through the air. The gold-friend of the Geats
did not boast of famous victories; his proven sword,
the blade bared in battle, had failed him
as it ought not to have done. That great Ecgtheow's
greater son had to journey on from this world
was no pleasant matter; much against his will,
he was obliged to make his dwelling
elsewhere — sooner or later every man must leave
this transitory life. It was not long
before the fearsome ones closed again.
The guardian of the hoard was filled with fresh hope,
his breast was heaving; he who had ruled a nation
suffered agony, surrounded by flame.
And Beowulf's companions, sons of nobles —
so far from protecting him in a troop together,
unflinching in the fight — shrank back into the forest
scared for their own lives. One man alone
obeyed his conscience. The claims of kinship
can never be ignored by a right-minded man.

His name was Wiglaf, a noble warrior,
Weohstan's son, kinsman of Ælfhere,
a leader of the Swedes;* he saw that his lord,
helmeted, was tormented by the intense heat.
Then he recalled the honours Beowulf had bestowed
on him — the wealthy citadel of the Wægmundings,
the rights to land his father owned before him.
He could not hold back then; he grasped the round,
yellow shield; he drew his ancient sword,
reputed to be the legacy of Eanmund,

* Wiglaf and his father Weohstan were also kinsmen of Beowulf. All
were members of the Wægmunding family.

Ohthere's son.
                    Weohstan had slain him
in a skirmish while Eanmund was a wanderer,
a friendless man, and then had carried off
to his own kinsmen the gleaming helmet,
the linked corslet, the ancient sword
forged by giants. It was Onela,
Eanmund's uncle, who gave him that armour,
ready for use; but Onela did not refer to the feud,
though Weohstan had slain his brother's son.
For many years Weohstan owned that war-gear,
sword and corslet, until his son was old enough
to achieve great feats as he himself had done.
Then, when Weohstan journeyed on from the earth,
an old man, he left Wiglaf — who was
with the Geats — a great legacy of armour
of every kind.
                    This was the first time
the young warrior had weathered the battle storm,
standing at the shoulder of his lord.
His courage did not melt, nor did his kinsman's sword
fail him in the fight. The dragon found that out
when they met in mortal combat.
    Wiglaf spoke, constantly reminding
his companions of their duty — he was mournful.
'I think of that evening we emptied the mead-cup
in the feasting-hall, partook and pledged our lord,
who presented us with rings, that we would repay him
for his gifts of armour, helmets and hard swords,
if ever the need, need such as this, arose.
For this very reason he asked us
to join with him in this journey, deemed us
worthy of renown, and gave me these treasures;
he looked on us as loyal warriors,
brave in battle; even so, our lord,
guardian of the Geats, intended to perform
this feat alone, because of all men

he had achieved the greatest exploits,
daring deeds. Now the day has come
when our lord needs support, the might
of strong men; let us hurry forward
and help our leader as long as fire remains,
fearsome, searing flames. God knows
I would rather that fire embraced my body
beside the charred body of my gold-giver;
it seems wrong to me that we should shoulder
our shields, carry them home afterwards,
unless we can first kill the venomous foe,
guard the prince of the Geats. I know
in my heart his feats of old were such
that he should not now be the only Geat to suffer
and fall in combat; in common we shall share
sword, helmet, corslet, the trappings of war.'
    Then that man fought his way through the fumes,
went helmeted to help his lord. He shouted out:
'Brave Beowulf, may success attend you —
for in the days when you were young, you swore
that so long as you lived you would never allow
your fame to decay; now, O resolute king,
renowned for your exploits, you must guard your life
with all your skill. I shall assist you.'
    At this the seething dragon attacked a second time;
shimmering with fire the venomous visitor fell on his foes,
the men he loathed. With waves of flame, he burnt
the shield right up to its boss; Wiglaf's
corslet afforded him no protection whatsoever.
But the young warrior still fought bravely, sheltered
behind his kinsman's shield after his own
was consumed by flames. Still the battle-king
set his mind on deeds of glory; with prodigious strength
he struck a blow so violent that his sword stuck
in the dragon's skull. But Nægling snapped!
Beowulf's old grey-hued sword
failed him in the fight. Fate did not ordain

that the iron edge should assist him
in that struggle; Beowulf's hand was too strong.
Indeed I have been told that he overtaxed
each and every weapon, hardened by blood, that he bore
into battle; his own great strength betrayed him.

    Then the dangerous dragon, scourge of the Geats,
was intent a third time upon attack; he rushed
at the renowned man when he saw an opening:
fiery, battle-grim, he gripped the hero's neck
between his sharp teeth; Beowulf was bathed
in blood; it spurted out in streams.
Then, I have heard, the loyal thane
alongside the Geatish king displayed great courage,
strength and daring, as was his nature.
To assist his kinsman, that man in mail
aimed not for the head but lunged at the belly
of their vile enemy (in so doing his hand
was badly burnt); his sword, gleaming and adorned,
sank in up to the hilt and at once the flames
began to abate. The king still had control then
over his senses; he drew the deadly knife,
keen-edged in battle, that he wore on his corslet;
then the lord of the Geats dispatched the dragon.
Thus they had killed their enemy — their courage
enabled them — the brave kinsmen together
had destroyed him. Such should a man,
a thane, be in time of necessity!

                          That was the last
of all the king's achievements, his last
exploit in the world. Then the wound
the earth-dragon had inflicted with his teeth
began to burn and swell; very soon he
was suffering intolerable pain as the poison
boiled within him. Then the wise leader
tottered forward and slumped on a seat
by the barrow; he gazed at the work of giants,
saw how the ancient earthwork contained

stone arches supported by columns.
Then, with his own hands, the best of thanes
refreshed the renowned prince with water,
washed his friend and lord, blood-stained
and battle-weary, and unfastened his helmet.
   Beowulf began to speak, he defied
his mortal injury; he was well aware
that his life's course, with all its delights,
had come to an end; his days on earth
were exhausted, death drew very close:
'It would have made me happy, at this time,
to pass on war-gear to my son, had I
been granted an heir to succeed me,
sprung of my seed. I have ruled the Geats
for fifty winters; no king of any
neighbouring tribe has dared to attack me
with swords, or sought to cow and subdue me.
But in my own home I have awaited
my destiny, cared well for my dependants,
and I have not sought trouble, or sworn
any oaths unjustly. Because of all these things
I can rejoice, drained now by death-wounds;
for the Ruler of Men will have no cause to blame me
after I have died on the count that I deprived
other kinsmen of their lives. Now hurry,
dear Wiglaf; rummage the hoard
under the grey rock, for the dragon sleeps,
riddled with wounds, robbed of his treasure.
Be as quick as you can so that I may see
the age-old store of gold, and examine
all the priceless, shimmering stones; once I
have set eyes on such a store, it will be
more easy for me to die, to abandon
the life and land that have so long been mine.'
   Then, I have been told, as soon as he heard
the words of his lord, wounded in battle,
Wiglaf hastened into the earth-cavern,

still wearing his corslet, his woven coat of mail.
After the fierce warrior, flushed with victory,
had walked past a daïs, he came upon
the hoard — a hillock of precious stones,
and gold treasure glowing on the ground;
he saw wondrous wall-hangings; the lair
of the serpent, the aged twilight-flier;
and the stoups and vessels of a people
long dead, now lacking a polisher,
deprived of adornments. There were many old,
rusty helmets, and many an armlet
cunningly wrought. A treasure hoard,
gold in the ground, will survive its owner
easily, whosoever hides it!
And he saw also hanging high
over the hoard a standard fashioned with gold strands,
a miracle of handiwork; a light shone from it,
by which he was able to distinguish the earth
and look at the adornments. There was no sign
of the serpent, the sword had savaged and slain him.
Then I heard that Wiglaf rifled the hoard
in the barrow, the antique work of giants —
he chose and carried off as many cups and salvers
as he could; and he also took the standard,
the incomparable banner; Beowulf's sword,
iron-edged, had injured
the guardian of the hoard, he who had held it
through the ages and fought to defend it
with flames — terrifying, blistering,
ravening at midnight — until he was slain.
Wiglaf hurried on his errand, eager to return,
spurred on by the treasures; in his heart he was troubled
whether he would find the prince of the Geats,
so grievously wounded, still alive
in the place where he had left him.
Then at last he came, carrying the treasures,
to the renowned king; his lord's life-blood

was ebbing; once more he splashed him
with water, until Beowulf revived a little,
began to frame his thoughts.
                                    Gazing at the gold,
the warrior, the sorrowing king, said:
'With these words I thank
the King of Glory, the Eternal Lord,
the Ruler, for all the treasures here before me,
that in my lifetime I have been able
to gain them for the Geats.
And now that I have bartered my old life
for this treasure hoard, you must serve
and inspire our people. I will not long be with you.
Command the battle-warriors, after the funeral fire,
to build a fine barrow overlooking the sea;
let it tower high on Whaleness
as a reminder to my people.
And let it be known as *Beowulf's barrow*
to all seafarers, to men who steer their ships
from far over the swell and the saltspray.'
    Then the prince, bold of mind, detached
his golden collar and gave it to Wiglaf,
the young spear-warrior, and also his helmet
adorned with gold, his ring and his corslet,
and enjoined him to use them well;
'You are the last survivor of our family,
the Wægmundings; fate has swept
all my kinsmen, those courageous warriors,
to their doom. I must follow them.'
    Those were the warrior's last words
before he succumbed to the raging flames
on the pyre; his soul migrated from his breast
to meet the judgement of righteous men.
    Then it was harrowing for the young hero
that he should have to see that beloved man
lying on the earth at his life's end,
wracked by pain. His slayer lay

there too, himself slain, the terrible
cave-dragon. That serpent, coiled evilly,
could no longer guard the gold-hoard,
but blades of iron, beaten and tempered
by smiths, notched in battle, had taken him off;
his wings were clipped now, he lay
mortally wounded, motionless on the earth
at the mound's entrance. No more did he fly
through the night sky, or spread his wings,
proud of his possessions; but he lay prostrate
because of the power of Beowulf, their leader.
Truly, I have heard that no hero of the Geats,
no fire-eater, however daring, could quell
the scorching blast of that venomous one
and lay his hands on the hoard in the lair,
should he find its sentinel waiting there,
watching over the barrow. Beowulf paid
the price of death for that mighty hoard;
both he and the dragon had travelled to the end
of this transitory life.
                    Not long after that
the lily-livered ones slunk out of the wood;
ten cowardly oath-breakers, who had lacked
the courage to let fly with their spears
as their lord so needed, came forward together;
overcome with shame, they carried their shields
and weapons to where their leader lay;
they gazed at Wiglaf. That warrior, bone-weary,
knelt beside the shoulders of his lord; he tried
to rouse him with water; it was all in vain.
For all his efforts, his longing, he could not
detain the life of his leader on earth,
or alter anything the Ruler ordained.
God in His wisdom governed the deeds
of all men, as He does now.
    Then the young warrior was not at a loss
for well-earned, angry words for those cowards.

Wiglaf, Weohstan's son, sick at heart,
eyed those faithless men and said:
'He who does not wish to disguise the truth
can indeed say that — when it was a question
not of words but war — our lord completely wasted
the treasures he gave you, the same war-gear
you stand in over there, helmets and corslets
the prince presented often to his thanes on the ale-bench
in the feasting-hall, the very finest weapons
he could secure from far and wide.
The king of the Geats had no need to bother
with boasts about his battle-companions;
yet God, Giver of victories, granted
that he should avenge himself with his sword
single-handed, when all his courage was called for.
I could hardly begin to guard his life
in the fight; but all the same I attempted
to help my kinsman beyond my power.
Each time I slashed at that deadly enemy,
he was a little weaker, the flames leaped
less fiercely from his jaws. Too few defenders
rallied round our prince when he was most pressed.
Now you and your dependants can no longer delight
in gifts of swords, or take pleasure in property,
a happy home; but, after thanes from far and wide
have heard of your flight, your shameful cowardice,
each of your male kinsmen will be condemned
to become a wanderer, an exile deprived
of the land he owns. For every warrior
death is better than dark days of disgrace.'
    Then Wiglaf ordered that Beowulf's great feat
be proclaimed in the stronghold, up along the cliff-edge,
where a troop of shield-warriors had waited all morning,
wondering sadly if their dear lord was dead,
or if he would return.
                    The man who galloped
to the headland gave them the news at once;

he kept back nothing but called out:
'The lord of the Geats, he who gave joy
to all our people, lies rigid on his death-bed;
slaughtered by the dragon, he now sleeps;
and his deadly enemy, slashed by the knife,
sleeps beside him; he was quite unable
to wound the serpent with a sword. Wiglaf,
son of Weohstan, sits by Beowulf,
the quick and the dead — both brave men —
side by side; weary in his heart
he watches over friend and foe alike.

Now the Geats must make ready for a time
of war, for the Franks and the Frisians,
in far-off regions, will hear soon
of the king's death. Our feud with the Franks
grew worse when Hygelac sailed with his fleet
to the shores of Frisia. Frankish warriors
attacked him there, and outfought him,
bravely forced the king in his corslet
to give ground; he fell, surrounded
by his retainers; that prince presented
not one ornament to his followers. Since then,
the king of the Franks has been no friend of ours.

Nor would I in the least rely on peace
or honesty from the Swedish people; everyone
remembers how Ongentheow slew Hæthcyn,
Hrethel's son, in battle near Ravenswood
when, rashly, the Geats first attacked the Swedes.
At once Ongentheow, Ohthere's father,
old but formidable, retaliated; he killed
Hæthcyn, and released his wife from captivity,
set free the mother of Onela and Ohthere,
an aged woman bereft of all her ornaments;
and then he pursued his mortal enemies
until, lordless, with utmost difficulty,
they reached and found refuge in Ravenswood.
Then Ongentheow, with a huge army, penned in

those warriors, exhausted by wounds,
who had escaped the sword; all night long
he shouted fearsome threats at those shivering thanes,
swore that in the morning he and his men would let
their blood in streams with sharp-edged swords,
and string some up on gallows-trees
as sport for birds. Just as day dawned
those despairing men were afforded relief;
they heard the joyful song of Hygelac's
horn and trumpet as that hero came,
hurrying to their rescue with a band of retainers.
After that savage, running battle, the soil
was blood-stained, scuffled — a sign of how
the Swedes and the Geats fomented their feud.
Then Ongentheow, old and heavy-hearted,
headed for his stronghold with his retainers,
that resolute man retreated; he realized
how spirit and skill combined in the person
of proud Hygelac; he had no confidence
about the outcome of an open fight with the seafarers,
the Geatish warriors, in defence of his hoard,
his wife and children; the old man thus withdrew
behind an earth-wall. Then the Swedes were pursued,
Hygelac's banner was hoisted over that earth-work
after the Geats, sons of Hrethel, had stormed
the stronghold. Then grey-haired Ongentheow
was cornered by swords, the king of the Swedes
was constrained to face and suffer his fate
as Eofor willed it. Wulf, the son
of Wonred, slashed angrily at Ongentheow
with his sword, so that blood spurted
from the veins under his hair. The old Swede,
king of his people, was not afraid
but as soon as he had regained his balance
repaid that murderous blow with interest.
Then Wonred's daring son could no longer
lift his hand against the aged warrior

but, with that stroke, Ongentheow had sheared
right through his helmet so that Wulf, blood-stained,
was thrown to the ground; he was not yet doomed to die
but later recovered from that grievous wound.
When Wulf collapsed, his brother Eofor,
Hygelac's brave thane, swung his broad sword,
made by giants, shattered the massive helmet
above the raised shield; Ongentheow fell,
the guardian of the people was fatally wounded.
Then many warriors quickly rescued Wulf,
and bandaged his wounds, once they had won control
(as fate decreed) of that field of corpses.
Meanwhile Eofor stripped Ongentheow's body
of its iron corslet, wrenched the helmet
from his head, the mighty sword from his hands;
he carried the old man's armour to Hygelac.
He received those battle adornments, honourably
promised to reward Eofor above other men;
he kept his word; the king of the Geats,
Hrethel's son, repaid Eofor and Wulf
for all they had accomplished with outstanding gifts
when he had returned home; he gave each of them
land and interlocked rings to the value
of a hundred thousand pence — no man on earth
had cause to blame the brothers for accepting
such wealth, they had earned it by sheer audacity.
Then, as a pledge of friendship, Hygelac gave
Eofor his only daughter to grace his home.

    That is the history of hatred and feud
and deadly enmity; and because of it,
I expect the Swedes to attack us
as soon as they hear our lord is lifeless —
he who in earlier days defended a land
and its treasure against two monstrous enemies
after the death of its heroes, daring Scyldings,
he who protected the people, and achieved feats
all but impossible.

Let us lose no time now
but go and gaze there upon our king
and carry him, who gave us rings,
to the funeral pyre. And let us not grudge gold
to melt with that bold man, for we have a mighty hoard,
a mint of precious metal, bought with pain;
and now, from this last exploit, a harvest
he paid for with his own life; these the fire
shall devour, the ravening flames embrace.
No thane shall wear or carry these treasures
in his memory, no fair maiden shall hang
an ornament of interlinked rings at her throat,
but often and again, desolate, deprived of gold,
they must tread the paths of exile,
now that their lord has laid aside laughter,
festivity, happiness. Henceforth, fingers must grasp,
hands must hold, many a spear
chill with the cold of morning; no sound of the harp
shall rouse the warriors but, craving for carrion,
the dark raven shall have its say
and tell the eagle how it fared at the feast
when, competing with the wolf, it laid bare the bones
    of corpses.'
    Thus the brave messenger told of and foretold
harrowing times; and he was not far wrong.
Those events were fated. Every man in the troop
stood up, stained with tears, and set out
for Eagleness to see that strange spectacle.
There they found him lifeless on the sand,
the soft bed where he slept, who often before
had given them rings; that good man's days
on earth were ended; the warrior-king,
lord of the Geats, had died a wondrous death.
But first they saw a strange creature
there, a loathsome serpent lying
nearby; the fire-dragon, fierce
and mottled, was scorched by its own flames.

It measured fifty paces from head to tail;
sometimes it had soared at night
through the cool air, then dived
to its dark lair; now it lay rigid in death,
no longer to haunt caverns under the earth.
Goblets and vessels stood by it,
salvers and valuable swords, eaten through
by rust, as if they had lain
for a thousand winters in the earth's embrace.
That mighty legacy, gold of men long dead,
lay under a curse; it was enchanted
so that no human might enter
the cavern save him to whom God,
the true Giver of Victories, Guardian of Men,
granted permission to plunder the hoard —
whichever warrior seemed worthy to Him.

Then it was clear that, whoever devised it,
the evil scheme of hiding the hoard under the rock
had come to nothing; the guardian had killed
a brave and famous man; that feud
was violently avenged. The day that a warrior,
renowned for his courage, will reach the end
(as fate ordains) of his life on earth,
that hour when a man may feast in the hall
with his friends no longer, is always unpredictable.
It was thus with Beowulf when he tracked down
and attacked the barrow's guardian; he himself
was not aware how he would leave this world.
The glorious princes who first placed that gold there
had solemnly pronounced that until domesday
any man attempting to plunder the hoard
should be guilty of wickedness, confined,
tormented and tortured by the devil himself.
Never before had Beowulf been granted
such a wealth of gold by the gracious Lord.
Wiglaf, the son of Weohstan, said:
'Many thanes must often suffer

because of the will of one, as we do now.
We could not dissuade the king we loved,
or in any way restrain the lord of our land
from not drawing his sword against the gold-warden,
from not letting him lie where he had long lain
and remain in his lair until the world's end;
but he fulfilled his high destiny. The hoard,
so grimly gained, is now easy of access;
our king was driven there by too harsh a fate.
I took the path under the earth-wall,
entered the hall and examined all
the treasures after the dragon deserted it;
I was hardly invited there. Hurriedly
I grasped as many treasures as I could,
a huge burden, and carried them here
to my king; he was still alive then,
conscious and aware of this world around him.
He found words for his thronging thoughts,
born of sorrow, asked me to salute you,
said that as a monument to your lord's exploits
you should build a great and glorious barrow
over his pyre, for he of all men
was the most famous warrior on the wide earth
for as long as he lived, happy in his stronghold.
Now let us hurry once more together
and see the hoard of priceless stones,
that wonder under the wall; I will lead you
so that you will come sufficiently close
to the rings, the solid gold. After we
get back, let us quickly build the bier,
and then let us carry our king,
the man we loved, to where he must
long remain in the Lord's protection.'
    Then the brave warrior, Weohstan's son,
directed that orders be given to many men
(to all who owned houses, elders of the people)
to fetch wood from far to place beneath

their prince on the funeral pyre:
                                                        'Now flames,
the blazing fire, must devour the lord of warriors
who often endured the iron-tipped arrow-shower,
when the dark cloud loosed by bow strings
broke above the shield-wall, quivering;
when the eager shaft, with its feather garb,
discharged its duty to the barb.'
    I have heard that Weohstan's wise son
summoned from Beowulf's band his seven
best thanes, and went with those warriors
into the evil grotto; the man leading
the way grasped a brand. Then those retainers
were not hesitant about rifling the hoard
as soon as they set eyes on any part of it,
lying unguarded, gradually rusting,
in that rock cavern; no man was conscience-stricken
about carrying out those priceless treasures
as quickly as he could. Also, they pushed the dragon,
the serpent over the precipice; they let the waves take him,
the dark waters embrace the warden of the hoard.
Then the wagon was laden with twisted gold,
with treasures of every kind, and the king,
the old battle-warrior, was borne to Whaleness.
    Then, on the headland, the Geats prepared a mighty pyre
for Beowulf, hung round with helmets and shields
and shining mail, in accordance with his wishes;
and then the mourning warriors laid
their dear lord, the famous prince, upon it.
    And there on Whaleness, the heroes kindled
the most mighty of pyres; the dark wood-smoke
soared over the fire, the roaring flames
mingled with weeping — the winds' tumult subsided —
until the body became ash, consumed even
to its core. The heart's cup overflowed;
they mourned their loss, the death of their lord.
And, likewise, a maiden of the Geats,

with her tresses swept up, intoned
a dirge for Beowulf time after time,
declared she lived in dread of days to come
dark with carnage and keening, terror of the enemy,
humiliation and captivity.
                                    Heaven swallowed the smoke.
    Then the Geats built a barrow on the headland —
it was high and broad, visible from far
to all seafarers; in ten days they built the beacon
for that courageous man; and they constructed
as noble an enclosure as wise men
could devise, to enshrine the ashes.
They buried rings and brooches in the barrow,
all those adornments that brave men
had brought out from the hoard after Beowulf died.
They bequeathed the gleaming gold, treasure of men,
to the earth, and there it still remains
as useless to men as it was before.
    Then twelve brave warriors, sons of heroes,
rode round the barrow, sorrowing;
they mourned their king, chanted
an elegy, spoke about that great man:
they exalted his heroic life, lauded
his daring deeds; it is fitting for a man,
when his lord and friend must leave this life,
to mouth words in his praise
and to cherish his memory.
Thus the Geats, his hearth-companions,
grieved over the death of their lord;
they said that of all kings on earth
he was the kindest, the most gentle,
the most just to his people, the most eager for fame.

APPENDICES

THE FINNESBURH FRAGMENT

The Finnesburh Fragment, like the Old High German *Hildebrandslied*, is all that survives of a Germanic 'lay' intended for recitation to the listening warriors in the hall. Professor Campbell tells us that 'lay employs a brief technique of narrative, with compressed description and rapid conversation, while epic expands in all three fields'. These characteristics can be seen in this Fragment if it is compared with any epic.

The story of the fight in Finnesburh in which Hnæf and his followers were attacked in a hall by their foes has been told in allusive fashion in *Beowulf*. It has given rise to much controversy. It is not clear exactly who began the fight, why they did, or when it took place. There is disagreement about how long the fight lasted. There are numerous other difficulties. But this much can be said in elucidation of the Fragment. Finn, King of the Frisians, has married the Danish princess Hildeburh, perhaps to patch up an existing feud between the two peoples. They have a son. While Hildeburh's brother Hnæf is visiting them at Finnesburh, he and his followers are surprised and treacherously attacked in their hall by Finn's retainers, possibly without his knowledge. At the end of the fight, Hnæf and his sister's son are both dead. It is generally (though not universally) agreed that the lay of which this Fragment forms part told of this battle. The *Beowulf* poet takes the story further and handles it with a different aim and emphasis; he uses the story to illuminate his poem and is concerned with the pathetic situation of Hildeburh, who has lost both son and brother, and with the tragic dilemmas of the other protagonists — Finn and the new Danish leader Hengest (identified by some with the Hengest who, according to the *Chronicle*, came to Britain with Horsa in 449). With him, the emphasis is on the 'pity (rather than the glory) of it all'.

But in the Fragment we feel the joy of battle. Here we have a situation which is brilliantly portrayed in another connexion by the

Beowulf poet — the dawn attack when the warriors in the hall, awakened, not by the sound of the harp to face a new day of happiness with their comrades, but by the foreboding cry of the dark raven, must start from their sleep to grasp the spear cold with the chill of morning. But the chill of the spear does not find its way to the hearts of Hnæf's followers. True to their code, they rush to the doors to fight against odds in defence of a narrow place — a typically heroic situation; compare the Spartans at Thermopylae, Horatius and his companions at the bridge, and Wulfstan and his at the causeway in *The Battle of Maldon*. Thus they repay the shining mead as well as men can; 'they held the doors . . .'.

THE FINNESBURH FRAGMENT

'. . . the gables are not burning.'
Then the young king spoke, a novice in battle:
'This light is not the light of dawn; no fiery dragon flies overhead;
The gables of this hall are not lit up with licking flames;
But men draw near with shining weapons. The birds of battle screech,
The grey wolf howls, the spear rattles,
Shield answers shaft. The pale moon wanders
On her way below the clouds, gleaming; evil deeds will now be done
Provoking pitched battle.
Wake up now, my warriors!
Grasp your shields, steel yourselves,
Step forward and be brave!'
So many a thane, ornamented in gold, buckled his sword-belt.
Then the stout warriors, *Sigeferth* and *Eaha*
Strode to one door and unsheathed their swords;
Ordlaf and *Guthlaf* went to guard the other,
And *Hengest* himself followed in their footsteps.
When he saw this, *Guthere* said to *Garulf*
That he would be unwise to go to the hall doors
In the first fury of the onslaught, risking his precious life,
For *Sigeferth* the strong was set upon his death.
But *Garulf*, a hero of great heart,
Shouted out, 'Who holds the door?'
'I am *Sigeferth*, a warrior of the Secgan
And a well-known campaigner; I've lived through many conflicts,
Many stern trials. Here, in strife with me,

You'll discover your fate, victory or defeat.'
Then the din of battle broke out in the hall;
The hollow shield, defender of the body, was doomed to disintegrate
In the hero's hand; the hall floor boomed.
Then *Garulf*, the son of *Guthlaf*, gave his life
In the fight, first of all the warriors
Living in that land, and many heroes lay prostrate beside him.
A crowd of pale faces fell to the earth. The raven wheeled,
Dusky, dark brown. The gleaming swords so shone
It seemed as if all Finnesburh were in flames.
I have never heard, before or since, of sixty triumphant warriors
Who bore themselves more bravely in the thick of battle.
And never did retainers repay their prince more handsomely
For his gift of glowing mead than did those men repay *Hnæf*.
They fought five days and not one of the followers
Fell, but they held the doors firmly.
Then *Guthere* retired, worn out and wounded;
He said that his armour was almost useless,
His corselet broken, his helmet burst open.
The guardian of those people asked him at once
How well the warriors had survived their wounds
Or which of the young men. . . .

TWO PASSAGES IN OLD ENGLISH

A. *Reading Instructions*

(i) Read slowly, pausing between half-lines according to the punctuation.

(ii) Follow generally the stress and intonation of Modern English. There are usually two main stresses in each half-line, one of which must fall on an alliterating syllable.

(iii) Vowels

> *a* and *ā* as in 'aha' respectively.
> *æ* and *ǣ* as in 'mat' and 'has' respectively.
> *e, i, o* as in Modern English.
> *u* as in 'pull' (NOT 'hut').
> *ē* as in 'hate'.
> *ī* as in 'seen'.
> *ō* as in 'goad'.
> *ū* as in 'cool'.
> *y* and *ȳ* as *i* and *ī*, with lips in a whistling position. (Cf. Modern French

tu and *ruse* respectively.)

Vowels in unstressed syllables should be pronounced clearly. This includes vowels at the end of words.

(iv) Diphthongs

> *ea, eo, ie* and *ēa, ēo, īe* may be pronounced as written.

But they are diphthongs, like the word 'I', not two vowels like *ea* in Le ander'.

(v) Consonants

> All consonants are pronounced. Double consonants are pronounced twice.

þ and *ð* = *th*.

> Most of the consonants are pronounced as they are today. The main exceptions are:

> *c* = *k*.
> *ċ* like *ch* in 'child'.
> *ġ* like *y* in 'yet'.
> *h* at the beginning of a word as in 'hound'.
> *h* otherwise like German *ch*.
> *sc* like *sh* in 'ship'.

B. *Lines 210–228. The Voyage to Denmark*

Old English Text (after Klaeber):

210 Fyrst forð ġewāt;   flota wæs on ȳðum,
     bāt under beorge.   Beornas ġearwe
     on stefn stigon, —   strēamas wundon,
     sund wið sande;   secgas bǣron
     on bearm nacan   beorhte frætwe,
215 gūðsearo ġeatolīċ;   guman ūt scufon,
     weras on wilsīð   wudu bundenne.

     Ġewāt þā ofer wǣġholm   winde ġefȳsed
     flota fāmīheals   fugle ġelīcost,
     oð þæt ymb āntīd   ōþres dōgores
220 wundenstefna   ġewaden hæfde,
     þæt ðā līðende   land ġesāwon,
     brimclifu blīcan,   beorgas stēape,
     sīde sǣnæssas;   þā wæs sund liden,
     eoletes æt ende.   Þanon up hraðe
225 Wedera lēode   on wang stigon,
     sǣwudu sǣldon, —   syrcan hrysedon,
     gūðġewǣdo;   Gode þancedon
     þæs þe him ȳþlāde   ēaðe wurdon.

Comment

   (i) Lines 210a–211a. Voyage not yet begun. Impression of solidity or stillness.

  (ii) Lines 211b–214b. Regularity of men moving backwards and forwards to ship on routine task. All half-lines four syllables.

 (iii) Lines 215–216. More syllables in each half-line. More stops — *g, t, k, w, d, b*. Impression of weight of ship. The word *ūt* in line 215b breaks half-line and gives grunt of effort.

 (iv) Lines 217–218. Again, more syllables than four in each half-line. Actual weight of half-lines very similar to (iii), but

Literal Gloss

> Time forth went; floater was on waves,
> boat under cliff. Warriors eager
> on prow climbed, — streams eddied,
> sea against sand; men bore
> into bosom of ship bright armour,
> war-gear splendid; men out shoved,
> warriors on wished-voyage wood [well-]bound.
> Went then over wave-sea by wind hastened
> floater foamy-necked to bird most like,
> until at due time of second day
> curved prow journeyed had,
> that the voyagers land saw,
> sea-cliffs shining, cliffs steep,
> wide sea-nesses; then was sea crossed,
> journey at end. Thence up quickly
> Geats' men on shore stepped,
> sea-wood moored, — mail shirts rattled,
> battle-garments; God [they] thanked
> because for them wave-paths easy had been.

many more continuants — *f, l, s, h, c.* Swift rocking movement of ship under sail with following wind, waves knocking against hull.

(v) Lines 219–224a. Settle down to regular rhythm and routine of voyage.

(vi) Lines 224b–225. Men moving again.

(vii) Lines 226–227a. Weight of ship and armour.

(viii) Lines 227b–228. Return to solidity. Voyage over.

(ix) Lines 221–223a. Accord with facts of sea-journey. You see land, then white shining cliffs, then individual headlands and promontories.

C. *Lines 2247–2266. The Lay of the Last Survivor*

Old English Text (after Klaeber):

'Heald þū nū, hrūse,   nū hæleð ne mōstan,
eorla æhte!   Hwæt, hyt ǣr on ðē
gōde beġēaton;   gūðdēað fornam,
2250 feorhbealo frēcne   fȳra ġehwylcne
lēoda mīnra   þāra ðe þis [līf] ofġeaf,
ġesāwon seledrēam.   Nāh, hwā sweord weġe
oððe fe(o)r(mie)   fǣted wǣġe,
dryncfæt dēore;   dug(uð) ellor s[c]eōc.
2255 Sceal se hearda helm   (hyr)stedgolde,
fǣtum befeallen;   feormynd swefað,
þā ðe beadogrīman   bȳwan sceoldon;
ġē swylce sēo herepād,   sīo æt hilde ġebād
ofer borda ġebræc   bite īrena,
2260 brosnað æfter beorne.   Ne mæġ byrnan hring
æfter wīġfruman   wīde fēran,
hæleðum be healfe.   Næs hearpan wyn,
gomen glēobēames,   nē gōd hafoc
ġeond sæl swingeð,   nē se swifta mearh
2265 burhstede bēateð.   Bealocwealm hafað
fela feorhcynna   forð onsended!'

Comment

This lament is spoken by the last survivor of a *comitatus*, the warrior-band of a king or great leader who led its members into battle and lavished gifts upon them in return for loyalty, even unto death. It commands attention from its dramatic introduction of the theme of transience to the concluding repetition of the same theme. From it we learn that the members of the *comitatus* shared a love of tried battle-gear and of the treasures won by those who wore it, a joy in

Literal Gloss

'Hold thou now, earth, now heroes have not been permitted,
nobles' possessions! Lo, it before from thee
good [men] won; war-death took away,
life-bale terrible of men each
of people mine of those who this life gave up,
[they] saw [the last of] hall-joy. I have none, who sword may carry
or may polish plated flagon,
drink-vat dear; doughty-band elsewhere went.
Must the hard helmet adorned with gold,
of ornaments [be] deprived; cleansers sleep,
those who battle-masks polish should;
also the mail-coat, which in battle endured
over shields' crashing [the] bite of swords,
decays after warrior. Nor may ring-mail
alongside war-leader widely journey
heroes beside. Not at all harp's joy,
mirth of song-wood, nor good hawk
through hall swings, nor the swift steed
fortress-yard beats. Bale-death has
many of human races forth on-sent!'

hawking, horse-riding, and fighting, and a communal pleasure in
music and feasting in the hall. Behind it we detect the spirit of
courage and fierce resolution which prompted their actions and the
isolation and misery of the last survivor who, deprived of all his
comrades and cut off from all that made life worth living, is left to
contemplate the now useless once-cherished possessions of his lost
friends. The forceful, almost tangible, images and the haunting
music of the passage can be left to speak for themselves.

INDEX OF IMPORTANT PROPER NAMES

For hints on pronunciation, see Appendix II.
On the Geatish–Swedish Wars, see Appendix VH.

Bēow, King of the Danes, son of Scyld.

Bēowulf, a Geat, hero of the poem.

Breca, chief of the Brondings, son of Bēanstān.

Dæghrefn, a Frankish warrior killed by Beowulf, probably in the battle in which Hygelac lost his life.

Ēadgils, Swedish prince, son of Ohthere. Helped by Beowulf (lines 2391–2396).

Ēanmund, brother of Eadgils. Killed by Wiglaf's father Weohstan (lines 2611–2625). Both the brothers were helped by Heardred (lines 2379–2390).

Ecglāf, a Dane, father of Unferth.

Ecgthēow, father of Beowulf, married Hrethel's daughter.

Eofor, a Geat who killed Ongentheow in battle (lines 2484–2489) and was rewarded with the hand of Hygelac's daughter in marriage (lines 2997–2998).

Finn, King of the Frisians. See Appendix VE.

Folcwalda, father of Finn.

Frēawaru, daughter of Hrothgar, married Ingeld.

Frōda, father of Ingeld.

Grendel, the monster killed by Beowulf.

Hæreth, father of Hygd.

Hæthcyn, Geatish prince, second son of Hrethel, who accidentally killed his elder brother Herebeald (lines 2435–2443). Killed in action by Ongentheow (lines 2481–2483) at Ravenswood (lines 2922–2941).

Hālga, Danish prince, father of Hrothulf.

Healfdene, King of the Danes, father of Hrothgar.

Heardrēd, Geatish king, son of Hygelac. Succeeded his father through Beowulf's loyalty (lines 2369–2379). Killed in action (lines 2202–2206) by Onela for helping Onela's rebel nephews (lines 2379–2390).

Helmings, the family to which Wealhtheow belongs.

Hengest, leader of the Half-Danes at Finnesburh after the death of Hnæf. See Appendix VE.

Heorogār, Danish king, elder brother of Hrothgar.

Heorot, hall of the Danish king Hrothgar.

Heoroweard, son of Heorogar.

Herebeald, Geatish prince, eldest son of Hrethel, accidentally killed by his brother Hæthcyn (lines 2435–2443).

Heremōd, King of the Danes. See Appendix VD.

Hererīc, probably uncle of Heardred and brother of Hygd.

Hildeburh, Danish princess, wife of the Frisian king Finn. See Appendix VE.

Hnæf, leader of the Half-Danes at Finnesburh. See Appendix VE.

Hōc, father of Hnæf and Hildeburh.

Hrēthel, King of the Geats, grandfather of Beowulf.

Hrēthrīc, son of Hrothgar.

Hrōthgār, King of the Danes in the time of Grendel.

Hrōthmund, son of Hrothgar.

Hrōthulf, Danish prince, nephew of Hrothgar, supposed by some to have seized the Danish throne after Hrothgar's death. See Appendix VE.

Hrunting, Unferth's sword.

Hūnlāfing, a warrior in Hengest's band.

Hygd, wife of Hygelac.

Hygelāc, King of the Geats. Beowulf is his sister's son, a particularly close tie among Germanic peoples. The ultimate victor at Ravenswood (lines 2941–2998). Killed in action (line 2201) in Frisia (lines 2354–2359) by the Franks (lines 2910–2921).

Ingeld, King of the Heathobards. See Appendix VG.

Mōdthryth, see Appendix VF.

Nægling, Beowulf's sword.

Ōhthere, son of the Swedish king Ongentheow.

Onela, King of the Swedes, son of Ongentheow. Married Healfdene's daughter (line 62). Killed by Eadgils (lines 2391–2396).

Ongenthēow, King of the Swedes. Rescued his wife at Ravenswood (lines 2928–2933). Subsequently trapped near Ravenswood and killed by Eofor (lines 2484–2489) and despoiled after striking down Eofor's brother Wulf (lines 2941–2998).

Scyld Scēfing, (mythical) Danish king. See Appendix VA.

Scyldings, the Danes, 'descendants of Scyld'.

Sigemund, famous Germanic hero. See Appendix VC.

Swerting, maternal uncle or grandfather of Hygelac.

Thryth, see Appendix VF.

Unferth, a courtier of Hrothgar.

Wǣgmundings, the family to which Weohstan, Wiglaf, and Beowulf belong.

Wealhthēow, Hrothgar's queen.

Wēland, in Germanic legend a famous maker of weapons.

Wīglāf, a Wǣgmunding and kinsman of Beowulf. A prince of the
Swedes (line 2603).

Wēohstān, father of Wiglaf, presumably a Swede (line 2603). Killed
Eanmund when fighting with Onela against Onela's nephews
(lines 2611–2619).

GENEALOGICAL TABLES

A. *The Danes*

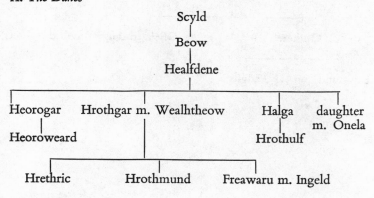

B. *The Geats*

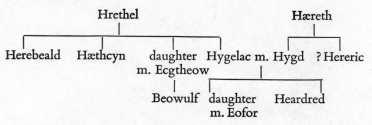

C. *The Half-Danes and The Frisians*

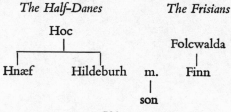

D. *The Heathobards*

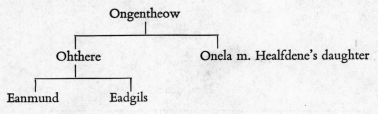

E. *The Swedes*

NOTES ON EPISODES AND DIGRESSIONS

Brief notes on the various episodes and digressions are given below. Those who believe that the poet was merely telling a story need not accept all the suggestions set out here. Many are arguable; see section 5 of the Introduction. For a detailed study of the digressions and their (possible) significance, see Adrien Bonjour, *The Digressions in Beowulf* (Oxford, 1950).

No attempt is made to distinguish the fabulous and supernatural elements from the historical. The distinction is a valid one for modern scholars (though the lines are often hard to draw), but it is by no means certain that Beowulf and the dragon were any less real to the poet and his audience than was the historical Hygelac.

A. *Scyld Scefing (lines 4–52)*

Scyld Scefing is presented by the poet as the eponymous hero of the Scyldings (the Danes). This is a natural beginning for a poem which goes on to tell about the Danes under Scyld's descendant Hrothgar, and it satisfies the Old English love of genealogies and their interest in origins. By glorifying the Danes, the story increases the seriousness of Grendel's threat and power, and so enhances Beowulf's deed.

Some see a parallel between Scyld and Beowulf — both come unexpectedly across the sea to save the Danes. A further parallel is sometimes detected. The poem begins with a leaderless people saved by a king whose magnificent funeral is described. It ends with the funeral of a king whose death leaves his people facing a time of peril. This gives the poem a cyclic movement which emphasizes that kings and empires, like everything else, rise and fall.

B. *The Burning of Heorot (lines 81–85 and 778–782)*

This seems a clear illustration of the technique (often attributed to the poet) of seeing what Miss Blomfield called 'the fruit in the seed'. Here the transience of earthly things is emphasized by the poet's reminder to his audience that the hall now towering in its newly-built majesty will ultimately suffer destruction by fire. That the exact circumstances of its destruction are not known for certain does not seem to me to affect this. (Some argue that it was burnt in the course of the Danish–Heathobard feud, others in the Danish civil wars which are supposed to have followed the death of Hrothgar. These are discussed in E. *The Finn Episode* below.) See further, section 5 of the Introduction.

C. *Sigemund* (lines 874–900)

Some see him as another illustration of the technique just discussed in B. above; see again section 5 of the Introduction.

D. *Heremod* (lines 901–915 and 1709–1724)

According to the genealogies, he was the Danish king before Scyld. After his death or exile — exactly what happened is not clear — the Danes were without a leader. Heremod is cited in Hrothgar's speech to Beowulf (lines 1709–1724) as a bad example, a man who failed to live up to the promise of his youth. Some think that the poet is contrasting Beowulf's slow beginning (lines 2183–2189) and his popularity and good end with Heremod's early promise and his final unpopularity and bad end.

Elsewhere in the poem the young Beowulf is portrayed as beginning well; see the account of the swimming contest with Breca (lines 506–586) and Beowulf's own report of the honour his grandfather King Hrethel did him while he was still a boy (lines 2426–2434). Such contradictions trouble only those who pursue an unjustified search for literal consistency; the poet is often concerned rather with the effect of the moment and is willing to use suitable material even if it does contradict something he has already said. Thus Hrothgar, after telling us in lines 1331–1333 that he does not know where Grendel's mother has taken her booty, goes on to describe the haunted mere where she and Grendel live (lines 1357–1379). We must therefore be chary of arguing from one passage that another passage must mean this or that.

Other problems seem to arise because the poet inherited certain details from an earlier version of the story without understanding their significance or without bothering to eliminate them. Possible examples are the curse on the dragon's gold (lines 3069–3075) and the burial by the Geats of the gold Beowulf won (lines 3163–3168).

All sorts of conflicting significances have been read into these two passages, but it is possible that the poet did not intend them to bear much weight. Study of the analogues (other versions of the same story) often helps us to recognize a problem but not always to solve it. We must remember that Old English poets probably had ideas about the structure of poems different from those held by modern critics. It is not without significance that almost all Old English poems are criticized in one way or another for their structure.

E. The Finn Episode (lines 1068–1159)

This incident is also treated in the independent *Fragment*, a translation of which will be found in Appendix I. For the family tree of those involved, see Appendix IVc.

What we know for certain about the incident can be summarized thus. A fight breaks out at Finnesburh through the treachery of the Jutes. In this fight Hnæf and his sister's son are killed. They are cremated on the same pyre. After this battle there is stalemate. Oaths are exchanged. Hengest, the new leader of the Half-Danes, is to serve Finn, who in his turn is to treat the Danes generously. Hengest spends the winter with Finn, brooding vengeance. Two Danish warriors, Guthlaf and Oslaf, rekindle the fight. Finn is killed in the second battle. The Danes return home with treasures and the thrice-bereaved Hildeburh.

The *Beowulf* poet does not tell the story in the straightforward manner of the *Fragment*, but in an allusive way which seems to assume that the audience knew it. But it does not follow from this that he must have had some elaborate purpose. He may have been content to call to mind the salient features of the story in a dramatic way. He tells in a Danish hall of a Danish victory and stresses the hopelessness of compromise in the face of tribal enmity — a situation of which he is rather fond. There are fine scenes and moments of high tragedy.

However, some think that it is more than a report of an heroic lay with which the *scop* entertained the company at the feast. These more subtle theories generally rest on the assumption that Hrothulf — brother's son to Hrothgar — treacherously seized the throne from Hrothgar's sons after their father had died. This assumption rests largely on two notions — that lines 1015–1019 and 1163–1165 imply that enmity ultimately broke out between Hrothgar and

Hrothulf and that there is dramatic irony in Wealhtheow's references to the loyalty of Hrothulf and the Danes in lines 1180–1187 and 1228–1231. These notions are possible but by no means certain deductions from the text. They are unsupported by any positive external evidence. Despite this, A. G. Brodeur writes with great assurance that 'no one doubts that these [the first] two passages forecast allusively the impending revolt of Hrothulf against his uncle and cousin, his murder of them, and his usurpation of the throne'. As we shall see later, at least one person does. But if we are swept along with this great tide of believers, what do we believe?

We believe that, just as Hildeburh was the victim of the treachery of the Jutes, so Wealhtheow is to be the victim of the (assumed) treachery of Hrothulf; that just as Hildeburh (it is assumed) was an unsuccessful 'peace-weaver' (line 1942), so the marriage of Freawaru, Hrothgar's daughter, to Ingeld King of the Heathobards will not patch up the Danish–Heathobard feud (see Appendix VG); and that, like Hengest, Ingeld will experience a conflict of loyalties which will be resolved by a call to action from his warriors. Thus we shall see the Finn Episode as a piece of dramatic irony which emphasizes that dynastic marriages cannot permanently resolve tribal enmities and contrasts the past successes and present happiness of the Danes with the troubles which will arise from the Danish–Heathobard wars in which Heorot is to be burnt (although, as we learn from the Old English poem *Widsith*, the Danes are ultimately successful) and from Hrothulf's subsequent treachery.

This is a brief amalgam of the sophisticated interpretations placed on this episode. But Kenneth Sisam has written:

The attitude of ordinary Anglo-Saxons to their heroic age is at issue in these interpretations. The occasion was a feast of rejoicing in the most famous of royal halls. Looking back on it, Beowulf, whose virtues included judgement and foresight, says: 'So King Hrothgar lived a good life' (2144), with no hint of internal trouble brewing. Yet according to one critic or another, Hrothulf was a traitor waiting for a chance to seize the throne by murdering his benefactors; Unferth too was a traitor trusted by both sides; Wealhtheow, fighting for the interest of her sons, suspected Hrothulf, and even Hrothgar's policy of 'adopting' Beowulf. How did this set of schemers get the reputation of heroes? Reading the text without gloss, I think the poet and his audience felt that the Heroic Age was more glorious than their own.

His question, I think, deserves an answer from what he calls 'whole-hearted admirers' of the structure of *Beowulf*. But I do not think that he has succeeded in demolishing their theories completely. He too has his assumptions — in particular 'that this kind of poetry depended on expression, not on silences, dark hints or subtle irony'.

F. *Thryth or Modthryth* (*lines 1931–1962*)

This is a difficult passage. It starts

Mōdþrȳðo wæg,
fremu folces cwēn, firen'ondrysne.

The first word can be taken as a proper name — 'Modthryth, bold queen of the people, displayed terrible wickedness'. It can be divided into two — *mōd* 'mood' and a proper name Thryth — 'Passion, terrible wickedness, possessed Thryth'. In either case, the digression is very abruptly introduced and is the most difficult of all for 'whole-hearted admirers' to justify. A few follow a recent theory advanced by Norman E. Eliason that there is no second queen and no digression; they take *mōdþrȳðo* as an abstract noun meaning 'arrogance' and think that the whole passage refers to Hygd. This seems to me doubtful. It is perhaps simplest to accept the existence of a digression, but to assume an omission in the manuscript. Those who claim that the digression as it stands has some purpose other than mere entertainment have not, in my opinion, produced any really satisfactory explanation.

G. *The Danish–Heathobard Feud* (*lines 2024–2069*)

The poet tells this story so clearly that it needs no recapitulation here. For a family tree of those involved, see Appendix IVᴅ. The story is put in the mouth of Beowulf on his return home to Geatland after killing Grendel and his mother. It has been explained as a prophecy by Beowulf of what will happen and as an account of something which was going on at Heorot while Beowulf was there. This latter view seems untenable; the poet gives us no hint. The best solution is probably that of A. G. Brodeur, who writes:

The poet was not concerned to tell the story of Ingeld as it was known already to his hearers; he wished to *use* it to illustrate Beowulf's wisdom and political insight. Accordingly he represents his hero, not as predicting what the audience knew had happened between Danes and Heathobards, but as seeing clearly the nature of the dangers which must threaten Hrothgar's hazardous policy, and as suggesting how unforeseen contingencies might bring disaster.

H. *The Geatish–Swedish Wars*

*For the relevant genealogical tables, see Appendix IV*B *and* E

The struggles between the Geats and the Swedes are not mentioned in lines 1–2199.* Lines 2200–3182 contain no digressions which are not concerned with them, and they are the first thing mentioned in this part of the poem:

> In later days, after much turmoil,
> things happened in this way: when Hygelac lay dead
> and murderous battle-blades had beaten down
> the shield of his son Heardred,
> and when the warlike Swedes, savage warriors,
> had hunted him down amongst his glorious people,
> attacked Hereric's nephew with hatred,
> the great kingdom of the Geats passed
> into Beowulf's hands.

The main stages of these wars can be set out thus:

(1) After the death of Herebeald and Hrethel, war breaks out between the Swedes and the Geats — perhaps started by the Swedes (lines 2472–2478).

(2) The Geats make an expedition of revenge against the Swedes (lines 2479–2480). A battle near Ravenswood falls into three stages (lines 2481–2489 and 2922–2998):

   (*a*) The Geats under Hæthcyn are at first successful; Ongentheow's queen is captured.
   (*b*) Ongentheow slays Hæthcyn and rescues his queen.
   (*c*) Hygelac's forces kill Ongentheow.

[Hygelac raids the Frisian territory of the Franks. He is routed and slain. Beowulf, after prodigies of valour, escapes by swimming. For line references, see the table below.]

* The death of Hygelac is mentioned in connexion with the wonderful jewel which is presented to Beowulf after he has killed Grendel (lines 1202–1214), but this was in a raid on the Frisian territory of the Franks. There are three (possibly four) mentions of his death in lines 2200–3182; see the table at the end of this Appendix.

(3) Heardred as King of the Geats gives refuge to Eanmund and Eadgils, the nephews of Onela, who has seized the Swedish throne. Onela slays Heardred and, through Weohstan (lines 2611–2625), Eanmund. Beowulf becomes King. Eadgils, assisted by the Geats, slays Onela and presumably becomes King of the Swedes (lines 2379–2396).

(4) The messenger fears further Geatish–Swedish wars on the death of Beowulf (lines 2999–3005):

> That is the history of hatred and feud
> and deadly enmity; and because of it,
> I expect the Swedes to attack us
> as soon as they hear our lord is lifeless.

And a Geatish woman, mourning at Beowulf's funeral pyre (lines 3150–3155),

> with her tresses swept up, intoned
> a dirge for Beowulf time after time,
> declared she lived in dread of days to come
> dark with carnage and keening, terror of the enemy,
> humiliation and captivity.

The poet nowhere gives a connected chronological account of these events. The table which follows contains line-references to all the passages where he refers to them.

	Death of Hygelac	*Geatish–Swedish Wars*
1	1202–1214	
2	2200–2206	
3	2354–2379	2379–2396
4	2490–2509*	2472–2489
5		2611–2625
6	2910–2921	2922–2998
7		2999–3005
8		3150–3155

Why did the poet introduce these stories? A. G. Brodeur gives a general judgement:

The historical traditions . . . deal with events conceived as falling within Beowulf's lifetime and personal observation or experience,

* Presumably this is relevant. Swedes (*Hugas*) are mentioned at lines 2502 and 2914.

and as touching him or his kinsmen directly. Though he is not
thought of as participating personally in all these historical events,
they are all of intense concern to him; those in which he is not
immediately involved affect the fates of personages who are his
friends or his foes. These historical stories give background and
setting for his later career; and their further function is dramatic and
vital: they are part of Beowulf's life.

Those interested in more detailed analysis of their possible significance should consult Adrien Bonjour, *The Digressions in Beowulf*
(Oxford, 1950), pp. 28–43.

SELECT BIBLIOGRAPHY

Editions

Beowulf and the Fight at Finnsburg, (ed.) Fr. Klaeber (3rd edn with Supplements, Boston, 1950).
Beowulf with the Finnesburg Fragment, (ed.) C. L. Wrenn (2nd edn, London, 1961).

Translations

Beowulf and the Finnesburg Fragment, a translation into Modern English prose, by J. R. Clark Hall, revised by C. L. Wrenn (London, 1950).
Beowulf, translated by David Wright (Harmondsworth, 1957).
Beowulf, A New Prose Translation, by E. Talbot Donaldson (London, 1967).
Beowulf, the Oldest English Epic, Translated into Alliterative Verse, by Charles W. Kennedy (New York, 1940).
Beowulf, A New [Verse] Translation, by Burton Raffel (New York, 1963).
Beowulf, A Verse Translation into Modern English, by Edwin Morgan (California, 1964).

Structure and Meaning

P. F. Baum, 'The *Beowulf* Poet', *Philological Quarterly* 39 (1960), 389–399.
N. F. Blake, Review of *The Structure of Beowulf* by Kenneth Sisam, *Medium Ævum* 35 (1966), 236–240.
Joan Blomfield (Mrs. Turville-Petre), 'The Style and Structure of *Beowulf*', *Review of English Studies* 14 (1938), 396–403.
Adrien Bonjour, *The Digressions in Beowulf* (Oxford, 1950).
Adrien Bonjour, '*Beowulf* and The Beasts of Battle', *Publications of the Modern Language Association of America* 72 (1957), 563–573.
A. G. Brodeur, *The Art of Beowulf* (California, 1959).

A. Campbell, 'The Old English Epic Style', in *English and Medieval Studies presented to J. R. R. Tolkien* (London, 1962).

H. Munro Chadwick, *The Heroic Age* (Cambridge, 1912).

Charles Donahue, '*Beowulf* and Christian Tradition: A Reconsideration from a Celtic Stance', *Traditio* 21 (1965), 55–116.

Norman E. Eliason, 'The "Thryth-Offa Digression" in *Beowulf*', in *Medieval and Linguistic Studies in Honour of Francis Peabody Magoun, Jr.* (London, 1965).

T. M. Gang, 'Approaches to *Beowulf*', *Review of English Studies* 3 (1952), 1–12.

G. N. Garmonsway, 'Anglo-Saxon Heroic Attitudes', in *Magoun Studies* (see above under Eliason).

Margaret E. Goldsmith, 'The Christian Theme of *Beowulf*', *Medium Ævum* 29 (1960), 81–101.

Margaret E. Goldsmith, 'The Choice in *Beowulf*', *Neophilologus* 48 (1964), 60–72.

W. P. Ker, *The Dark Ages* (London, 1904).

W. P. Ker, *Medieval English Literature* (Oxford, 1912).

John Leyerle, 'Beowulf the Hero and the King', *Medium Ævum* 34 (1965), 89–102.

John Leyerle, 'The Interlace Structure of *Beowulf*' (A memorial lecture for the late Professor Norman Garmonsway), *University of Toronto Quarterly* 37 (1967), 1–17.

F. P. Magoun, Jr., '*Beowulf* B: a folk-poem on Beowulf's Death', in *Early English and Norse Studies Presented to Hugh Smith* (London, 1963).

M. B. McNamee, S.J., '*Beowulf* — An Allegory of Salvation?', *Journal of English and Germanic Philology* 59 (1960), 190–207.

Karl Müllenhoff, *Beovulf* (Berlin, 1889).

Alain Renoir, 'Point of View and Design for Terror in *Beowulf*', *Neuphilologische Mitteilungen* 63 (1962), 154–167.

Kenneth Sisam, 'Beowulf's Fight with the Dragon', *Review of English Studies* 9 (1958), 129–140.

Kenneth Sisam, *The Structure of Beowulf* (Oxford, 1965).

E. G. Stanley, '*Beowulf*', in *Continuations and Beginnings* (London, 1966).

Benjamin Thorpe, *The Anglo-Saxon Poems of Beowulf The Scop or Gleeman's Tale and The Fight at Finnesburg* (Oxford, 1855).

J. R. R. Tolkien, *Beowulf: The Monsters and the Critics* (Sir Israel Gollancz Memorial Lecture, British Academy, 1936).

J. R. R. Tolkien, 'The Homecoming of Beorhtnoth, Beorhthelm's Son', *Essays and Studies* 6 (1953), 1–18.

William Whallon, 'The Idea of God in *Beowulf*', *Publications of the Modern Language Association of America* 80 (1965), 19–23.

Sources and Analogues

R. W. Chambers, *Beowulf, an Introduction to the Study of the Poem with a Discussion of the Stories of Offa and Finn*, 3rd edn with Supplements by C. L. Wrenn (Cambridge, 1959; reprinted 1963).

See also the editions of Klaeber and Wrenn.

Metre and Appreciation of the Verse

A. J. Bliss, *The Metre of Beowulf* (Oxford, 1958).

Alan Bliss, *An Introduction to Old English Metre* (Oxford, 1962).

A. G. Brodeur, *The Art of Beowulf* (California, 1959).

Randolph Quirk, 'Poetic language and Old English metre', in *Early English and Norse Studies Presented to Hugh Smith* (London, 1963).

E. G. Stanley, '*Beowulf*', in *Continuations and Beginnings* (London, 1966).

J. R. R. Tolkien, 'Prefatory Remarks' to the Wrenn–Clark Hall translation.

Recordings

Beowulf and Other Poetry in Old English, read in Old English by J. B. Bessinger, Jr. (Caedmon Records No. 1161). This is obtainable from the College Department, Houghton Mifflin Co., 53 West 43rd St., New York, N.Y., 10036.

The Argo Recording Company plans to publish two records of extracts from *The Battle of Maldon and Other Old English Poems* and from this translation.

Archaeology and Art

E. A. Fisher, *An Introduction to Anglo-Saxon Architecture and Sculpture* (London, 1959).

Charles Green, *Sutton Hoo* (London, 1963).

D. M. Wilson, *The Anglo-Saxons* (London, 1960).

History

Bede, *A History of the English Church and People*, translated by Leo Sherley-Price (Harmondsworth, 1955).

P. Hunter-Blair, *An Introduction to Anglo-Saxon England* (Cambridge, 1956).

F. M. Stenton, *Anglo-Saxon England* (2nd edn, Oxford, 1947).

Dorothy Whitelock, *The Audience of Beowulf* (Oxford, 1951).

Dorothy Whitelock, *The Beginnings of English Society* (Harmondsworth, 1952).

Literature

Stanley B. Greenfield, *A Critical History of Old English Literature* (New York, 1965; London, 1966).

C. L. Wrenn, *A Study of Old English Literature* (London, 1967).

The Battle of Maldon and Other Old English Poems, translated by Kevin Crossley-Holland and introduced by Bruce Mitchell (London, 1965).

Grammar

A. Campbell, *Old English Grammar* (Oxford, 1959; reprinted with corrections 1962).

Bruce Mitchell, *A Guide to Old English* (Oxford, 1965; 2nd edn, 1968).

[This book contains a more detailed Select Bibliography.]